CHRONICLES OF
RELIGIOUS SCIENCE

THE HISTORY OF THE
RELIGIOUS SCIENCE MOVEMENT,
WITH INTERVIEWS, QUOTES,
AND COMMENTARY
NOV. 1926 – FEB. 2012

RESEARCHED, COMPILED, AND EDITED BY

Dr. Marilyn L. Leo

FOREWORD BY

Rev. Dr. John Waterhouse

SCIENCE OF MIND
ARCHIVES & LIBRARY FOUNDATION
Where the Past Illuminates the Future

SCIENCE OF MIND ARCHIVES & LIBRARY FOUNDATION
GOLDEN, COLORADO

For further information on Science of Mind, visit Science of Mind Archives & Library Foundation at http://scienceofmindarchives.org. 573 Park Point Drive, Golden, Colorado, 80401, phone: (720) 496-1361, or via email at info@somarchives.org.

Composition and manufacturing by CreateSpace.
Book design by Deborah Freeland.

Published by Science of Mind Archives & Library Foundation
573 Park Point Drive
Golden, CO 80401
http://scienceofmindarchives.org

ISBN 978-0-9897300-0-6

First printing, July 2013.

Printed in the United States of America.

Table of Contents

Acknowledgements

First and foremost, I want to acknowledge the living divine Presence within me for the ideas, the outline, and the cover of this book. Next, for the many friends who encouraged and supported my endeavor and helped in many ways in the development of this project.

Among them was James Abbott, now manager of the Science of Mind Archives and Library, who helped during my many visits to the Archives in Golden, Colorado for research; Claudia Abbott, for sharing her home with me while I stayed in Colorado; the Dr. John Hefferlin and Marian Hefferlin Foundation Board members for their confidence and financial support for the necessary travel; Arthur Vergara for his time, willingness, and patience to review my manuscript and offer suggestions; Shirley Morgan, RScP, and other volunteers in the Archives; to the many people who gave me encouragement when the project seemed overwhelming; and the more than forty persons who took their time to share their stories with me.

My deep gratitude and appreciation goes to Mr. Steve Burton, Operations Manager of Centers for Spiritual Living. He (along with Dr. Steve Gabrielson, Dr. Jim Lockard, and Dr. John Waterhouse) has provided me with his journal and accounting of the integration process that took place from before 2010 through February 2012, the year of the final integration. We know there will be many more adjustments and compromises made, but in generations to come there, will be fewer concerns and questions about how "the split" came about; conversations will only be about the reuniting that took place. We will be known simply as Centers for Spiritual Living (CSL), teaching Science of Mind, universal principles, the philosophy of Ernest Holmes, and the wise ones of the ages.

Special thanks to the volunteers who helped to research during the editing of the book: Melinda Eskridge, Laurie Hendren, and Donna Fisk, and to Deborah Freeland for her devotion in editing this book.

And to all the Science of Mind students, who gave me a reason for researching one hundred forty-seven years' worth of Board minutes and our history, thank you.

Bless you all.

Rev. Marilyn Leo, D.D., R.Sc.D.

Foreword

One hundred years ago, a young man named Ernest Holmes, who grew up in turn-of-the-century New England, was beginning his career as a teacher, lecturer, and philosopher in Southern California. In the ensuing years, a spiritual movement emerged through his efforts and those of many others who called him "teacher." As a result, the lives of untold numbers around the world have been inspired and their spiritual awareness deepened. Even though there have been numerous changes in the organizational structures within Religious Science, the basic tenets of our faith remain constant as well as the central focus of our existence as a world-class spiritual movement.

Chronicles of Religious Science tells the interesting story of how this spiritual movement has progressed over its first century. Those of us who have evolved spiritually and prospered greatly from Dr. Holmes's work and the rich wisdom that he synthesized into what we call "Science of Mind" will greatly appreciate the depth of historical understanding that emerges from these *Chronicles*.

There is no one better, more knowledgeable, or more committed to creating this historical review than Dr. Marilyn Leo. Having had a deeply personal relationship with Dr. Holmes as family friend, neighbor, and teacher, Dr. Marilyn has been a chief observer of the evolution of Religious Science throughout her life. Her father, Reginald Armor, became a student of Dr. Holmes when he was a teenager and was among his closest advisors throughout the formation of the Institute of Religious Science and beyond. Dr. Marilyn has also been the long-time guardian of many organizational records and documents and is the founder of the Science of Mind Archives and Library Foundation. I am deeply grateful for the extraordinary amount of time and energy she has invested in bringing these *Chronicles* to fruition.

The *Chronicles* Dr. Marilyn presents are, of course, not a complete history of all Religious Science organizations. Over the years, vast amounts of printed material has been amassed, including organizational minutes, resolutions, and bylaws, along with personal correspondence, newsletters, and much more. What the *Chronicles of Religious Science* provides is a series of narrative snapshots, extrapolated from these thousands of documents and personal remembrances, and reported through interviews that reveal many of the most important moments of growth, change, celebration, and sorrow that have occurred along the way.

Some might assume that a historical review would be somewhat dry, but that has not been my experience with the *Chronicles*. Within these chapters are extraordinary revelations, some causing me to laugh and others prompting me to shake my head in disbelief, since hindsight is always "20/20." Most of these events are described in one or two short paragraphs and are tied together as though one were looking through a photo album, seeing the progression of change over time. For me, the exploration of these actions and experiences by my predecessors was an enriching experience that strengthens my resolve to give my very best as a leader within our movement.

The subjects Dr. Marilyn presents are of major interest, discussed repeatedly at Board meetings and involving issues such as how money was raised, spent, borrowed, and repaid. Board actions also included the purchase and sale of major commercial investments, many of which would not be possible today, given current nonprofit restrictions. The *Chronicles* also reveal several major challenges with churches, teaching chapters and individuals, along with organizational name changes and the processes of those changes.

In the development of her book, Dr. Marilyn conducted many interviews with people who attended the 1954 Convention of the International Association of Religious Science Churches—at which the infamous "split" occurred—as well as with others who have participated in organizational leadership by serving on boards, committees, and in the creation and development of the Holmes Institute, the League of Practitioners, global centers, youth programs, and all levels of course curriculum.

Chronicles of Religious Science begins in 2012 by recalling the events and activities that established Centers for Spiritual Living, focusing particularly on the combining of membership and resources of United Church of Religious Science (d.b.a. United Centers for Spiritual Living) and International Centers for Spiritual Living (formerly known as Religious Science International and earlier as International Association of Religious Science Churches) into one new, preeminent organization, and the largest in the history of the Religious Science movement.

Chapter 2 returns to the establishment of Religious Science in 1926 and moves forward through a chronology that depicts all major milestones occurring along the way. Because of the many important events of the 1950s, Chapter 5 is subdivided into three distinct parts: before the split, the events of the split, and how the two organizations moved forward after the split.

2000 to 2010 were years filled with changes for United Church of Religious Science and Religious Science International. These changes had a major influence on the direction of both organizations, bringing us again to 2012, when Religious Science is reestablished under a unified banner and organizational structure that is committed to bringing Science of Mind more fully to the world.

Throughout history, many churches and religious organizations have had divisions and separations. Such incidents are only mildly newsworthy. However, the reunification of major factions within a spiritual movement is far rarer and allows our organization the opportunity of becoming a substantial spiritual influence in the world. Centers for Spiritual Living, as an integrated organization, has developed a new and powerful synergy that will certainly cause the teaching of Science of Mind to expand, influencing the consciousness of people around the world by teaching them that "there is a Power for good in the Universe, greater than you are, and you can use It."

Anyone wanting to understand and experience the ups and downs of our collective journey—anyone who feels a sense of gratitude for all the energy, effort, money, and creative initiative it has taken over the last century to bring these teachings to us individually and collectively—will benefit from reading this compilation of events and remembrances. I have enjoyed the journey thoroughly, and I'm certain you will as well.

Rev. John B. Waterhouse, Ph.D.
President, Centers for Spiritual Living
Co-Founding Minister, Center for Spiritual Living, Asheville, North Carolina

Preface

You can't really know where you're going until you know where you've been.

Alex Hitchens (character in *Hitch*, 2005)

My purpose in writing this book has been to compile in one volume, as concisely and as accurately as possible, an overview of the history and development of the Religious Science Movement. To this end, one hundred forty-two years of Religious Science Board minutes and correspondence were reviewed, and more than forty interviews conducted.

It has been a labor of love, and it may well be that parts of the story have been unintentionally missed. In my research, I found instances where no mention was made in the minutes of the beginnings or the conclusion of a particular project, and, on other occasions, found no trace of the minutes of meetings that had obviously been held.

A great many people have played an important part in the Movement's development. The following pages detail their role and influence as well as comprehensive information on the Movement's growth and culture.

From the early beginnings in 1926, the minutes reveal that some activities have remained constant: financial restructurings have occurred; properties and stocks have been bought and sold; global activities have been pursued; and changes have been made to the educational curriculum. In addition, we get a glimpse of the birth of the Holmes Institute, changing business practices, major upsets in the organization, the development and growth of the *Creative Thought* and *Science of Mind* magazines, practitioners' associations, the evolution of ministry, and other subjects that will be of interest to the reader.

The main subject of this book is not Ernest Holmes, the Movement's founder, or the philosophy of Science of Mind. Rather, the focus is on the development of the organization that was created to spread and teach Science of Mind principles and their practical applications as envisioned and perceived by Holmes.

For the reader interested in knowing more about Ernest Holmes, currently available books include: *That Was Ernest* and *Ernest Holmes the Man*, by Reginald Armor; *Ernest Holmes, His Life and Times*, by Fenwicke Holmes; *Open at the Top, the Life of Ernest Holmes*, by Neal Vahle; *The Inner Light*, reprinted as *Your Aladdin's Lamp*, by William H. D. Hornaday and Harlan Ware; *The Holmes Papers* in three volumes by George Bendall; and, *In His Company: Ernest Holmes Remembered*, by Marilyn Leo.

And so now, with an open mind and with appreciation, let's look first at the current picture of the Religious Science Movement, now known as the Centers for Spiritual Living. We will then look at how it all began and follow its history to the present day.

Marilyn Leo

CHRONICLES OF RELIGIOUS SCIENCE, VOLUME 1

1

We've Come a Long Way, Baby!
Where We Are Now
2010 – Present 2012

*Of course I know the whole thing will come back together when
the right time comes, merely because it is the logical thing to do
and I think in the long run, common sense usually wins.*

Ernest Holmes, excerpt from a letter to Raymond Charles Barker,
March 8, 1960 [one month before Holmes's transition]

It may not be all that important what our Religious Science ancestors did or
did not do in the development of the Religious Science movement, but this
is the story of how it all started and where we are now. Over the generations,
there has been a maturity reached, whereas only twenty years ago, there
was some doubt whether the Religious Science movement would last much
longer.

We have now come together to create a strong and vibrant energy that
many believe will at long last be the greatest impulsion of humankind. That
was Ernest Holmes's belief: "Religious Science is the next great impulsion in
the world." That "next" is the *present*. There is a wonderful story to be told, a
philosophy to be shared, and a practical application of universal principles
to be practiced called the Science of Mind.

In February 2011, a great new movement was created. What was thought
could not happen, happened. What became two paths in the 1950s resumed
its way, making one giant road in the New Thought movement and the
world of religion. On the one hand the Institute of Religious Science and

Philosophy, the Church of Religious Science, the United Church of Religious Science, and the United Centers for Spiritual Living, and on the other hand the International Association of Religious Science Churches, Religious Science International, and the International Centers for Spiritual Living have rejoined forces and become Centers for Spiritual Living. At the 2011 Leadership Conference held in San Diego, California, the Bylaws, Articles of Incorporation, and Organizational Design Model were overwhelmingly approved by the many hundreds of delegates in attendance. To bring this to fruition took hundreds of hours with hundreds of people willing to work toward this integration. This will be the story of Chapter 1. Are we, then, beginning with the end? No; we are beginning with the new beginning of a new organization and a renewed global spiritual movement.

INTEGRATION FINALLY TAKES PLACE

Was it two years, four years, or decades that United and International have been in the process of coming together, of reuniting as one? The answer is: "All of the above."

For decades, going back as far as the early 1960s, there have been leaders and visionaries who said that if we are to teach oneness, we must *be* one. There were many attempts and several false starts over the last fifty years.

In New Orleans, Louisiana, on Monday, February 13, 2012 (Valentine's Day Eve), a combined 640 delegates of International Centers for Spiritual Living (ICSL) and United Centers for Spiritual Living (UCSL), with each delegate serving a secondary role as delegates for Centers for Spiritual Living (CSL)—met at the Sheraton Hotel on Canal Street.

On that date, at 1:00 P.M., the delegates quickly passed several amendments to the Bylaws and Organizational Design Model (ODM) with nearly unanimous support of each amendment. By early afternoon, the delegates were voting on ratification of the new 164-page Policies and Procedures that would serve as the foundation for how CSL would soon be conducting its daily operations. By 4:00 P.M., it was time to elect the first president of Centers for Spiritual Living.

The field of candidates was an impressive list of four very qualified ministers: Dr. Kathianne Lewis, Dr. Jim Lockard, Dr. John Waterhouse, and Dr. Petra Weldes. No candidate received the required 40-percent-plus-one proportion of votes, so a run-off election was held immediately after the votes had been tallied. Dr. Jim Lockard and Dr. John Waterhouse were the two candidates with the most votes. Each was given five minutes to address the conference; the delegates again cast their votes.

One by one, delegates walked down the center aisle and placed their ballots in the ballot box. In an adjacent room, the tabulation committee was busy counting the ballots. In the end, Dr. John Waterhouse received 52 percent of the vote, making him the first President of Centers for Spiritual Living. By 6:00 P.M., the delegates had heard from two powerful candidates for Spiritual Leader, Rev. Dr. Harry Morgan Moses and Dr. Kenn Gordon. Each demonstrated a passion for bringing our organization's spiritual message to the world. The votes were cast, and Dr. Gordon was elected to serve as the first Spiritual Leader of Centers for Spiritual Living.

Later that week, twenty-three other elections were held by electronic voting. The organization's first Leadership Council was elected with three ministers: Dr. Heather Clark, Dr. Patrick Cameron, and Rev. David Alexander; three practitioners: Becky Moore, Deborah Gauvreau, and Drew Johnson; and three laity members: Walter Drew, Geoffrey Sindon, and Eileen Flannigan. Additionally, the delegates elected six members to serve on the first Practitioner Council: Linda Watson, Baji Daniels, Jeanette Vinek, Deborah Ford, Marianne Giblin, and Susan Pahnke; and the newly formed Laity Council had six newly elected members: Paul Hietter, Pam Lambert, Jeff Hagins, Mari Avicolli, Susan Hopkins, and Layne Taylor. The delegates also elected Karen Fry, RScP, as Candidate Search Committee Chair of the Nominations Council and Dr. Sandy Jacob as Qualifications Committee Chair for the Nominations Council.

THE BEGINNINGS OF INTEGRATION

Twelve months earlier, the delegates of both organizations had met in San Diego to determine whether the three governing documents—Bylaws, Organizational Design Model, and Affiliation Agreement—would be adopted. On Monday, February 28, 2011, the delegates spent six hours hearing debates and voting on amendments to the three documents. Those that passed were inserted in the documents; the next morning, the delegates voted by paper ballot. The historic vote on all three documents solidified oneness in the form of Centers for Spiritual Living by passing in both organizations; 97 percent voted to approve the Organization Model, the Bylaws, and the Affiliation Agreement. Such high approval might give one the idea that this had been an easy—even effortless—decision. However, this assumption would be totally wrong.

The thought of becoming one organization started to gain momentum in March of 2003 when Rev. Jim Lockard sent a six-page memo titled "One Mind, One Heart, One Voice" to both Dr. Kathy Hearn, Community Spiritual Leader of United Church of Religious Science, and the Board of Directors of

Religious Science International. In that memo, Rev. Lockard laid out both the reasons for becoming one organization and his thoughts on how it could be done.

His opening vision statement read:

THE VISION:

It is time. It is time to act, to take the steps necessary to create a single voice for Religious Science by acting to heal "the split." The issues of forty-nine years ago are not our issues today. We have grown in consciousness and in organizational sophistication. We can accommodate greater diversity within a single organization today. We can take the steps in action which already exist in consciousness—we can unite. It is time to make the decision to do so. If it was not clear before, our experience in Scottsdale [Arizona] confirmed it for most of us. The idea is right and the time is NOW.

From this memo, the first Visioning Bridge Committee met in Los Angeles. The meeting was attended by Dr. Kathy Hearn, Dr. David Walker, Dr. Petra Weldes, Dr. Sandy Jacob, Eileen Flannigan, Dr. Jim Turrell, Rev. Nirvana Gayle, and Rev. Jim Lockard.

Over the next five years, the committee met two to three times a year and more often by conference calls. Meetings were held at Mile Hi Church in Lakewood, Colorado; Seaside Church in Escondido, California; and San Juan Capistrano, California. Other ministers joined the committee, including Dr. Candice Becket, Dr. Heather Clark, Rev. Sandy Moore, Dr. Sue Rubin, Rev. Roger Juline, Rev. Madalyn Wade, Rev. Karen Weingard, and Dr. John Waterhouse.

During these meetings, the group discussed what one organization would look like, how it would operate, and how to take these ideas to the next level.

In July 2007, Religious Science International (later to become International Centers for Spiritual Living) voted to authorize their Board of Directors to pursue a merger with United Church of Religious Science (d/b/a United Centers for Spiritual Living).

In September of the same year, the Religious Science International Board of Directors and the United Church of Religious Science CORE Council met at the Los Angeles Marriott Hotel to discuss the possibility of a merger. The meeting was facilitated by Rev. Deborah Johnson; she suggested that instead of calling the objective a "merger," it be called "integration." From that point, the process was referred to as Integration.

2008 was a pivotal year. The Visioning Bridge Committee met in San Juan Capistrano, California. Following this meeting, an Integration Summit was planned. It convened on September 11, 2008. This event, held at the Los Angeles Marriott and facilitated by Rev. Deborah Johnson, was attended by approximately 300 representatives from Religious Science communities all across North America.

The Integration Summit was a major turning point toward Integration. Some in attendance met people from the other organization for the first time, and everyone experienced firsthand the possible value of being one organization. After the Summit, the Visioning Bridge Committee renamed itself the Integration Team.

Less than three months later, on November 24 and 25, an Education Summit convened at the Los Angeles Marriot. Everyone realized that education was among the highest priorities if we were to effectively integrate our organizations. A second meeting followed with ongoing communication between the two organizations' departments of education. Dr. Jeffery Proctor was a key player in this coming-together, until his passing only days after the second education meeting.

Long before any of these activities were conceived, the youth were actively expressing Oneness. They did this by keeping alive the question, "Why are we separate organizations if we teach Oneness?" As youth often do, they became the example of Oneness and began holding joint camp retreats in 2000.

This caused event leaders from both organizations to take notice; in January 2009, a meeting was held at United's headquarters in Golden, Colorado. Those present from ICSL were Rev. Jim Lockard, Dr. Steve Gabrielson, Rev. Pat Campbell, Dr. Kenn Gordon, Rev. Frankie Timmers, Rev. Karen Wolfson, and Tammi Tucker. From UCSL were Dr. Judy Morley, Dr. Kathy Hearn, Rev. Ron Fox, and Rev. Denise Schubert. Also attending the meeting was Melanie Marconi representing BDI, an event- planning and management company that had been used by UCSL in the past. The meeting was a success, but the greatest outcome was having the two organizations work together to combine their annual meetings, including Asilomar in the summer and a joint conference that would host ICSL's annual Congress and UCSL's annual Community Gathering. Both the Congress and the Gathering were business meetings of the organizations where annual state-of-the-organization addresses and financial reports were given, and, of course, amendments and resolutions voted on. The 2010 conference became another pivotal point in the history of Integration.

The leadership of both organizations realized that to make Integration a reality, it would need structure, financial resources, staffing, and a lot of time and effort. At the time, no one realized just how much time, talent, and money would be required to bring Integration to fruition over the next three and a half years.

PLANNING BEGINS IN EARNEST

In the spring of 2009, Dr. Kathy Hearn called a strategic planning meeting with the Leadership Team of UCSL. They met at the home of Rev. Jerry Fetterly in Lakewood, Colorado. Along with Dr. Hearn and Rev. Fetterly, Dr. Judy Morley, Rev. Gregory Toole, and facilitator Cindy Henson attended the meeting. Although the intended purpose of the meeting was for UCSL strategic planning, something felt out of place. The team realized that everything would be influenced by Integration, so Dr. Hearn called for a strategic planning session at the UCSL offices in Golden, Colorado that would include leaders from ICSL. She contacted Dr. Kenn Gordon, president of ICSL, inviting him to bring a core group of representatives. Those representing ICSL were Dr. Kenn Gordon, President; Dr. Steve Gabrielson, Vice President; Dr. Karen Kushner, Vice President; Dr. Candice Becket, Director of Youth; and Dr. Jim Lockard, Transformation Director. Representing UCSL were Dr. Kathy Hearn, Community Spiritual Leader; Dr. Michelle Medrano, CORE Council Chair; Dr. John Waterhouse, CORE Council Secretary; Rev. Gregory Toole, Ecclesiastical Leader; Dr. Judy Morley, Communications Leader; and Steve Burton, Operations Leader. The meeting was facilitated by Cindy Henson of Henson and Associates. Everyone quickly realized that the work of this group of individuals was to foster the design and implementation of a new organization.

The outcome of this first meeting of the combined leadership was the creation of the goal of integration as one organization. At the suggestion of Dr. Kathy Hearn, the group named itself the Design Team. Dr. John Waterhouse drafted an initial timeline for the work of this team that culminated with the election of officers in early 2012. A great deal of work would be required to meet this goal, but the group of leaders, with their broad array of skills and experience, was up to the task of ushering in Integration.

The task of the Design Team soon became increasingly clear. The greatest hurdle was to overcome the cultural differences that had developed over their fifty-plus years of separation. While each organization embraced and taught the same Science of Mind philosophy, and all called themselves Religious Scientists, each group conducted their affairs and governed themselves quite differently. Their educational approaches to teaching Science of Mind were different, and the roles of ministers and practitioners evidenced wide variances between the two cultures.

A second meeting was scheduled for the following month. Dr. Kathianne Lewis offered to host the Design Team at Center for Spiritual Living, Seattle, Washington. Rev. Gregory Toole suggested that we start with a cocreation process so that we could begin by focusing on healing the rift that had existed for more than half a century between the two cultures. Everyone who had attended the first meeting in Golden was at the meeting in Seattle. The work began with a cocreation process led by Dr. Marcia Sutton.

As part of the process, Dr. Kenn Gordon read a letter found in the ICSL archives a few days earlier. It was from Dr. Ernest Holmes to Dr. Raymond Charles Barker, and read in part:

I am sure your interest is in the permanency of the movement, the same as mine is, even though we are on two sides of the same coin. Of course, I know the whole thing will come back together when the right time comes, because it is the logical thing to do, and I think, in the long run, common sense usually wins.

Dr. Gordon also read from the document signed by Dr. Holmes and all parties who had formalized the agreement to separate into independent organizations. As part of the process, those present ceremonially envisioned a healing for each person by name.

The process was a great success, and from that meeting several key factors emerged. First and foremost was the Design Team's willingness to oversee a complex and voluminous amount of work that would require a hands-on approach from the leadership of both organizations. The group agreed to share leadership, and the team concept would be to design a new organization that the delegates of both organizations could approve.

The Design Team began meeting by phone at 10:00 A.M. PST every Wednesday. Over the next two years, this team would explore virtually every aspect of the new organization, working with hundreds of volunteers who were giving of their talents and thousands of hours of their time.

Also at the Seattle meeting, an organizational consultant, Dr. Steven Gomes, made a presentation on how he could support the two organizations in coming together. In July 2009, at the Sheraton San Diego Hotel and Marina, he led the ICSL Board of Directors through a preliminary discovery process regarding the steps and benchmarks that would be addressed over the coming months. In early August, Dr. Gomes facilitated the same process with the UCSL CORE Council at Asilomar State Park in Pacific Grove, California.

Following the CORE Council meeting with Dr. Gomes, Steve Burton telephoned Dr. Steve Gabrielson at his office in Newport Beach, California. After an hour-long discussion, it became apparent that the complexity of this integration could not and would not fit into a corporate-merger matrix. There was no internal fix after more than fifty years.

The following week, the annual UCSL Summer Conference at Asilomar was to take place. ICSL had already had their weeklong retreat (this was a tradition that predated the split). During that week, Steve worked with Dr. Michelle Medrano and Dr. Petra Weldes on bylaws amendments that would need to be voted on and passed at the UCSL Gathering the following February in Denver. These amendments would gauge the mood of the community members with regard to Integration and were crucial in moving the process forward. Dr. Steve Gabrielson crafted amendments for the same purpose at ICSL.

Also that week, Steve Burton developed a reverse timeline starting with an integrated organization in February 2012 and working backward to identify everything that would need to be accomplished from September 2009. The concept that Steve Burton and Steve Gabrielson (who became known as "the two Steves") developed was to divide the major aspects of the organizations into separate areas of focus and assign each to a Module Team for review and collaboration on a plan for Integration in that area.

MODULE TEAMS ARE FORMED

When the Integration Plan was launched in spring 2010, there were 18 Module Teams; and members of either organization could serve on any two of these teams. These were working volunteer groups, the wisdom behind limiting participation to two teams being that volunteers would stay focused and not burn out. The eighteen teams are listed in a table on page 9.

The Module Teams worked diligently, and each group brought great value to the whole. However, the area that caused the most concern was how to address ministerial education effectively, particularly given how vastly different the two approaches were. The discussions among team members Dr. Karen Kushner, Dr. Lynn Connolly, Dr. Kim Kaiser, Dr. Deborah Gordon, Dr. Carol Carnes, and Rev. Gregory Toole were difficult at times, not so much because individuals didn't want change, but because each organization saw ministerial education as very connected to the core of who they were and what they wanted to honor in their culture and identity. A great deal of

Module Team	Focused On
Global Heart Vision/ Guiding Principles	Organizational Culture
Governance Integration Ombudsman	Leadership Structure & Roles, Cores/Committee
Organization Structure	Voting Procedures, Bylaws, Organizational Design Model, Member Relations/Structure & Requirements
Communications	Publications, Branding, Marketing, Websites, Public Relations Outreach
Finance	General Development, Foundation, Retirement
Spiritual Practices	Vision CORE, Prayer-Partnership, Practitioner Support for the Organization, Musician Ministry Support
Spiritual Outreach	World Ministry of Prayer, Online Practitioner Support
Strategic Alliances/ Global Engagement	Strategic Alliances, United Clergy of Religious Science, International Core
Transformation	Research & Development, New Ideas
SOMARK, Inc.	Trademarks, Branding
Professional Standards	Licensing & Credentialing, Awards & Honorary Doctorates, Ceremonies & Protocol/Etiquette, Ethics, Organizational Mediation & Peacemaking, Church/ Center Charters
Youth	Camps, Advisor/Teacher/Facilitator Certification, Youth Curriculum, Youth Programs/Center Support, Youth Governance
Administration Structure & Roles	Staffing/Office Location, Legal & Other Professional Services, Information Technology
Field Organization, Structure & Roles	Field Representatives, Growth & Development Issues Support, Center Support, Membership, Covenant/ Affiliation Agreements, Laity Organization, Interim Ministry Program
Practitioner Organizations	Practitioners Council
Growth & Development	Center Development, New Works Support
Conferences & Events	Future Conferences
Education	Online Education, Accredited/Certified Classes, Practitioner Training, Ministerial Training, Professional Development Training

surrender and letting go was required as team members listened intently to one another, asked questions, and persistently stayed with the process. There were many times when the team felt it had reached agreement and found resolution only to discover when presenting the model to broader focus groups that the two organizations were still far apart on this subject. Person by person, question by question, and issue by issue, this team stayed together until there were no major issues remaining. The team's effort resulted in a plan that was accepted by the Design Team; it then went to the Board and Core of the two organizations for their approval. By honoring the highest values held by each organization, the team had done what many thought impossible.

In March of 2010, once amendments were passed by the delegates of both ICSL and UCSL, the Module Teams began their work, every aspect of which needed to be completed by August 1, 2010. The work of each Module Team would first be reviewed by an Editorial Team, and the Design Team would then make the final review before sending the documents to the ICSL Board of Directors and the UCSL CORE Council by October 2010. Once approved by both governing bodies, the documents would be placed on both of the organizations' ballots. It was an aggressive and tight timeline with little room for missteps.

The two Steves agreed to meet in Los Angeles following Asilomar. In the lobby of the LAX Radisson, they worked on details for many hours. During one of their first teleconference meetings, in September, the reverse timeline was presented to the Design Team for approval. Steve Burton led the presentation and took the team through the complete process before entertaining questions or comments. Steve Burton, Dr. Judy Morley, and Rev. Gregory Toole were together in the conference room during the call. After the presentation, Steve asked for questions or comments. They were greeted with absolute silence from those on the teleconference line—the three looked at each other in alarm, and Steve said in alarm, "We lost the connection!" Dr. John Waterhouse quickly responded, "No! We are just in shock."

It began to sink in how monumental an undertaking this was going to be for the team. Every Module Team would have one or two Design Team members on it, often serving as the chair of the Module Team. Dr. John Waterhouse recommended that activities and progress on the plan be communicated through an online system called Basecamp. This would become the project management software used by the Module Teams and the Design Team as a central repository of notes and conversations. Rev. Leigh Waddel served as the administrator, keeping everyone trained and the team's activities posted. Leigh's involvement kept everyone on track throughout the process.

Each of the Module Teams had its own personality, and each operated slightly differently. The functionality of Basecamp was clear in the first meeting of the Governance Module in early March 2010 (the first Module Team to form). Within minutes, members became aware of how differently things were done in one organization or the other. The two Steves were chairing this team, and both realized that a different approach was needed. They asked each member to write about the history of how governance had been handled in ICSL and UCSL, and to post it to Basecamp. After that experience, everyone felt heard, and there was a much greater openness to understanding the differences between the two cultures.

The other approach that was used when two individuals had strong—even passionate—views that were in conflict was to have the people with opposing views work together over the following week, posting the results of their conversations on Basecamp. Almost always, the conflict would be resolved and a solution found by the next weekly conference call.

Conference calls became the major method of communication during the integration process. Throughout 2010 and most of 2011, the average number of weekly Integration conference calls for each Design Team member was between fifteen and twenty-five.

The Module Team process would begin in March 2010. Participants from both organizations would first meet at the joint conference held in February at the Sheraton Convention Center in downtown Denver. It was a very successful conference, with both organizations having separate business meetings and all other events shared under the leadership of the joint event committee.

At that conference, United passed with no problems the amendments that would enable integration to proceed. International had a more interesting meeting; Chris Yamas, a youth representative, came to the microphone and stated that the youth were already integrated, and it was past time for the organizations to follow suit. He was followed by Dr. Jim Turrell, who made a motion for the entire integration process to be put on hold for three years to allow for more discussion. Unsurprisingly, this caused a lot of conversation, with many others stepping forward to speak in support of integration. It was Dr. Elizabeth Marshall who put the discussion to bed when she addressed the delegates and said that she had been at the meeting that caused the split. She said, "It was wrong then, it's wrong now, and it's time to come together as one." After her words of wisdom, there was a call for the vote, and the motion to suspend integration received just one vote.

While United's integration conversation was far less interesting, the financial report included an announcement about the United Clergy Retirement Plan, which was underfunded by $12.5 million, and the prospects of certain bankruptcy if actions were not taken immediately. Steve Burton led that conversation with the delegates, and later that day, he held a meeting with Plan participants and the members of the Retirement Committee, Dr. Roger Juline and Dr. Ruth Deaton. Later that year, the plan itself was retired by paying out over $12 million to the participants in lump-sum amounts. A spirit of cooperation was truly revealed through the wisdom and understanding of the Plan participants, who expressed trust rather than anger and upset as the Plan was closed.

On Thursday of the conference, Dr. John Waterhouse and Dr. Jim Lockard led an "Open Space" process in which delegates worked in small groups to talk about what they wanted to see in the new organization. After that exercise, many participants became members of one or more Module Teams.

In March 2010, the Module Teams were launched and the work began. Each week, the Design Team met by phone once and sometimes twice to discuss progress and areas of concern, and to monitor for issues.

In June 2010, Dr. Michelle Medrano formed a team that had the role of bringing all of the Module Teams' recommendations together into one of two documents—the Organizational Design Model or the Bylaws. Her team included Rev. Andy Torkelson, Dr. Petra Weldes, Steve Burton, Walter Drew, Loretta Huss, and Gina MacLean. Their mission was to review the work of the Module Teams and to break it down into parts that were to go into the ODM and other parts that were to go into the Bylaws. This work continued into mid-August. Their drafts were sent to the Design Team as two separate documents.

The Design Team met in late August at a hotel near Denver International Airport and spent three days working through every line of the ODM and Bylaws. Several important debates ensued; some sections were rewritten, and new sections were added to express new or expanded ideas. The three tedious days were facilitated by Susan LeTurneau, a professional facilitator and member of Mile Hi Church in Lakewood, Colorado.

Out of this meeting, a third document—the Member Community Affiliation Agreement—was created. Its purpose was to create an agreement of understanding between the organization and each community member by framing the responsibilities of one to the other.

A final revelation of the Design Team was the need for one more cocreation process before the San Diego conference to work on any remaining differences. That meeting took place at the LAX Radisson Hotel in January 2011, and it was facilitated by Rev. Penny Macek.

Up to this point in the process, no lawyers had been involved to give legal advice, completely contrary to the way most corporate mergers work. However, the time had come for a full legal review, and the two Steves were tasked with pulling together a strong legal team. Neither Steve Burton nor Dr. Steve Gabrielson was a lawyer, and they would co-chair the team. The rest of the team was made up of lawyers who were also Religious Scientists and practicing in various fields of law or retired from practice. This team included Geoffrey Sindon, Dr. Tom Sannar, Rev. David Lowe, Rev. C. C. Coltrain, Bob Gordon, and Paul Skok, RScP. They were given a window of one month to review all three documents, discuss them, and submit recommendations back to the Design Team. The team had a standing conference call every week with many urgent calls in between as members worked in teams to review specific sections. One conference call ran over six hours. Nevertheless, the team got the job done and sent its recommendations to the Design Team, which implemented most of their suggestions.

On October 27 through 29, 2010, the ICSL Board of Directors and the UCSL CORE Council convened a joint meeting at the Red Lion Hotel in Spokane. During those two days of meetings, the combined leadership of the two organizations reviewed the proposed Bylaws, ODM, and Affiliation Agreement; with the Design Team, all of whom were members of one governing body or the other, they answered questions from the combined group. In the end, all the members of both governing bodies voted to place the documents on the February ballot.

For a new organization to be formed, the passage of the ODM, Bylaws, and Affiliation Agreement was crucial. So, between November 2010 and January 15, 2011, Dr. Kenn Gordon and Dr. Kathy Hearn traveled to ten cities and held area "town hall" meetings, in which they explained the intentions of our new Centers for Spiritual Living and provided an overview of the documents that would make it a reality. The Design Team also held a series of informational conference calls with the delegates to answer any questions they might have. Between the town-hall meetings, conference calls, and information packets, the delegates attending the San Diego conference would be some of the best-informed people in either organization's history.

THE SAN DIEGO CONFERENCE

During the week of February 27 to March 4, 2011, the delegates arrived at the Sheraton San Diego Hotel and Marina for a historic vote. Monday, February 28 began at 8:00 A.M. with each organization holding regular business meetings, hearing a few presentations, and exchanging financial reports. The real meeting began in the afternoon, with delegates gathering in a large ballroom. ICSL delegates entered from the left, and UCSL delegates entered from the right. Dr. Kenn Gordon and Dr. Kathy Hearn made a presentation regarding the process and acknowledged the hundreds of volunteers and thousands of hours that had gone into the documents upon which the attendees would be voting.

Dr. Randy Crutcher was introduced as the facilitator—or, as he put it, "traffic cop" for the day. The meeting and the voting process had been planned by the Design Team, under the direction of the two Steves, with the intention of completing the floor discussions in one afternoon. Different scenarios were in place that would place the vote as early as Tuesday and as late as Thursday, with the understanding that the most likely scenario was for the process to take all of Monday afternoon and most of Tuesday, hearing amendments and debate, and voting on amendments to the documents, and then voting to accept the documents as amended on Wednesday.

Dr. Crutcher laid out the rules for presenting amendments, making comments, or asking questions. The room was set to move through the process quickly and still allow all voices to be heard. The next step was a question-and-answer session, with the Design Team giving the answers. For all but a few of the questions, Steve Burton answered on behalf of the Design Team. What most people didn't see was the teamwork going on among the Design Team, from members passing notes to Dr. Jim Lockard sitting next to Steve with all of the color-coded documents and quickly finding what a speaker was referring to in his or her question or comment and passing it to Steve.

After a short break, Dr. Crutcher opened the floor to amendment proposals; there were several. Each amendment would pass or fail based on a standing vote of the delegates. Paper ballots were ready to be issued, but were never needed. Rev. Joe Hooper introduced three "packages" of amendments totaling over twenty amendments. The first two packages failed, and Rev. Hooper withdrew the third package. There were amendments from the youth, practitioners, and delegates concerning various phrases or wording. By 4:30 P.M., it appeared that the business could be completed that day if there were no dinner break. So, a quick order for six hundred sandwiches went out, and the hotel made it happen on short notice. The meeting was adjourned at 6:30 P.M., with all work completed and ready for the vote on Tuesday morning.

On Tuesday morning, at 8:00 A.M., the doors opened for voting. Each organization had a separate voting area in the ballroom, and there were separate Teller Committees to oversee the voting process. Voting was done by paper ballot, and two long lines of people were at the door at 8:00 A.M. ready to cast their ballots. By noon, the Teller Committees were tabulating. A notice went out to all delegates to reconvene at 4:00 P.M. for the results. The delegates cast votes overwhelmingly in favor of the documents, averaging 97 percent approval (97 percent, 96 percent, and 98 percent, respectively) for each of the three documents (Bylaws, Organizational Design Model, and Community Affiliation Agreement). The delegates broke out in celebrations, and the room was filled with excitement, accomplishment, and—to some—a sense of loss, as the new organization would replace what had been two great organizations.

INTEGRATION IS COMPLETED

For many, the work was over, but the Design Team was only halfway to the finish line. It was now time to address the details. From the earliest draft of the reverse timeline, and always present in the minds of the Design Team, the formation of Centers for Spiritual Living would occur in two parts over two years. The 2011 vote would be the "big picture," focused on the documents that governed who Centers for Spiritual Living would be and, in general, how it would operate. The 2012 vote would be the adoption of the Policies and Procedures, which evolved into a 142-page manual. The other significant task of the 2012 conference would be to elect the first leaders of Centers for Spiritual Living. This included the Spiritual Leader, president, nine Leadership Council members, six Practitioner Council members, six Laity Council members, and two co-chairs of the Nomination Council.

To make this work, an aggressive schedule would again need to be followed. The Design Team used the format of the previous year and created Development Teams in place of Module Teams. Creating Policies and Procedures for areas such as licensing, credentialing, and education was an enormous undertaking that would require the establishment of many different teams under the leadership of Dr. Karen Kushner and Rev. Gregory Toole. All aspects of the organization were identified and assigned to Development Teams for the creation of appropriate policies and procedures. This stage of development would also include creating a new employee handbook (Employee Resource Guide) to implement the changes that staff would see in the new organization.

The Design Team looked at the compensation packages of both organizations and found that both failed to meet what the Design Team felt was needed to support a professional staff. So, a committee was formed and a consultant was hired to review both organizations' pay and benefit structures. Then, the median salary for nonprofit and for-profit companies of comparable size nationwide was researched. Following the adoption of the consultant's recommendations, the salaries and benefits were adjusted on March 1, 2012, the first official business day of Centers for Spiritual Living.

Fall 2011 was very hectic as the Policies and Procedures Development Teams submitted work to the Review Team, led by Dr. Michelle Medrano, who performed content evaluation on the Development Teams' progress. The team then released each section for legal review, and all approved sections were sent to Gina MacLean and Geoffrey Sindon to be assembled into a comprehensive manual. This final draft was reviewed over a two-day period by the ICSL Board of Directors and the UCSL CORE Council, which met in Spokane in November. At that meeting, the document was approved with minor revisions and prepared for a vote for ratification by the delegates in New Orleans.

While these efforts were taking place, the Nominating Team was recruiting qualified candidates for Centers for Spiritual Living leadership positions. This team was co-chaired by Dr. Sandy Jacob (ICSL) and Practitioner Becky Moore (UCSL). Every Wednesday morning, Dr. Jacob, Becky, Gina MacLean, Dr. Steve Gabrielson, and Steve Burton met by conference call to review the status of different candidates being vetted to ensure they were qualified to hold the offices to which they had been nominated. Discussions included updates on the candidate website, designed and administered by Rev. Leigh Waddel, and on other important election issues.

In January 2012, there were ten candidate conference calls in which delegates who would be attending and voting at the conference could ask questions of the candidates. These calls were organized by specific positions. Four calls were for the combined candidates of Spiritual Leader and President, two calls for the candidates for Leadership Council, two calls for the Practitioner Council, and two calls for the Laity Council. The candidates for nominations were available for the Practitioner Council and the Laity Council phone calls. In total, there were sixty-four candidates for twenty-five elected positions. Steve Burton facilitated the calls by inviting questions or reading questions that had been received from delegates via email. The calls were informative, well-attended, and at times quite humorous. Gina MacLean was controlling the system and serving as timekeeper, and the first few calls were a challenge because even though delegates had been asked to mute their phones, background noises and comments often caught the attention of the other participants. On the second call, Steve repeatedly asked that everyone mute their phones. He finally said, "Would whoever is watching *Wheel of Fortune* please mute your phone?" New Orleans was just a few days away when the last conference call occurred.

A New Way of BeingMuch more could be written on the Integration of these two organizations. It was unorthodox, a grassroots process designed from the bottom up. Much of what was created came forth as a third way—a new way—of being in our organization. In the corporate world, a merger often occurs in days or weeks, and there is almost always a "winner" and a "loser." One organization takes over the other's culture, and the surviving company moves on. This Integration process was different, not least because it was designed to allow everyone to participate.

The new entity—Centers for Spiritual Living—is comprised of the best of both its originating organizations, and it brings forth the best culture and process that each had to offer. It has been a process of "letting go and letting God." Through this process, great bonds of friendship and love have been created that will endure the challenges that this new organization will face.

It was worth the many years, the more than $250,000 invested, the tens of thousands of volunteer hours, and all the talents, skills, and emotions that were shared to bring Integration to pass.

2

The 1920s:
When It All Began

*In the beginning was the Word, and the Word
was with God and the Word was God.*

The Holy Bible, King James, John 1:1

No, I'm not suggesting that Ernest Holmes created the earth, sun, moon, stars, and so forth. But he did create the Science of Mind teaching. He studied the great philosophers and thinkers of history and found a thread of Truth that ran through all of their teachings and writings. Holmes brought forth this Truth for all generations to come, and made it understandable. He created a legacy. He learned that his word, as well as everyone else's word, had power— the power to create—and he taught us how to direct this power for good.

THE BEGINNING

For ten years or so before the formal creation of the Institute of Religious Science and School of Philosophy in 1927, Holmes was speaking to hundreds of people in California and on the East Coast. He was a modern-day philosopher, and many later called him a mystic. He read literature daily concerning all fields of science, religion, psychology, philosophy, art, and music. He spent many more hours in contemplation, meditation, and writing.

Holmes was especially popular in Southern California (his home), entertaining engineers, scientists, university professors, ministers, celebrities in the movie industry, and executives of major companies. In his early years, he took elocution lessons from Leland Powers while living in Boston,

Massachusetts, and his timing, voice control, and diction with a slight New England accent—as well as his charisma and his novel ideas—were highly respected and enjoyed.

On one of his trips returning to the East Coast to lecture and teach classes, Ernest hired a secretary, Ann Shipman, to take down in shorthand what he said as he gave classes and lectures. In time, he edited those words, and by 1926, he had created what became known as *The Science of Mind* textbook. It was his cousin, Idella Chadwick, who brought it all together, and it was copyrighted in his mother's name, Anna Holmes. *The Science of Mind*, published by Robert M. McBride in New York (today by Tarcher-Penguin Group), has had many printings, as many thousands of copies have been read around the world, but there have been only two editions—the second was published in 1938.

During these early years, as students were being trained in class by Ernest Holmes, Anna ("Mother") Holmes and Reginald Armor served as practitioners. Healing groups were formed.

· 1926 ·

CREATING A CORPORATION

In the latter part of 1926, a group of men came together to form a corporation based on the teachings of Holmes. On December 10, 1926, they held their first formal meeting in the office of Clinch & Thurtle Real Estate, prominent real-estate dealers in Los Angeles, at 503 S. Western Avenue, Los Angeles, California. The following eight men were officially named as the "Board of Governors" of the organization: Ernest Holmes; Mostyn C. H. Clinch, of Clinch & Thurtle; Lem A. Brunson, known as "the Deacon," one of the developers of the Santa Fe Springs oil district and a developer of Bel Air, an exclusive area of Los Angeles; Robert L. Hendry, a friend of Brunson in the oil-well supply business; Frank B. Hathaway, retired from the Hathaway School for Underprivileged Children and a humanitarian; J. Farrell MacDonald, a character actor and hero of the silent films; Harrison Lewis, Beverly Hills businessman; and Reginald Armor, a very young man who had been a close associate of Holmes's since age twelve in 1915. Though Holmes was named as a member initially, he did not want to be a member of the Board of Governors and did not accept the official leadership of the Board. He said, "My job is to deliver the water of Life, to keep it flowing. Your task is to post the signs showing people where to find it." Clinch was elected chairman, Hathaway treasurer, and Lewis secretary.[1]

This being their first meeting, it was moved that the organization be incorporated; it was suggested that the members of the Board consult with an attorney. Holmes, Clinch, and MacDonald were asked to "investigate further and report on permanent headquarters."[2] Holmes was also asked to make arrangements for a permanent lease of the Theatre Room at the Ambassador Hotel.[3]

During the next several months, many decisions were made regarding the setup of the organization. These included the decision about who would sign checks. Clinch was authorized to engage the law offices of Jones, Wilson, & Stephenson in Los Angeles to proceed with the incorporation of the organization. The first annual meeting and banquet was proposed to be held on January 19, 1927 at the Elks Club at 6th St. and Lake St., Los Angeles, California. The cost per plate was $2.50. The Entertainment and Program Committees were appointed; these tasks were usually handled by the wives of the Board members, and these women were put in charge of arranging the entertainment for the evening. A committee of ten men and ten women was appointed as a reception committee on the evening of the banquet.[4]

At the December 22, 1926 meeting, it was verbally agreed that Holmes would "accept the leadership of the organization for an indefinite period over a number of years, adequate salary to be arranged for by [the] Board of Governors at a later meeting."[5] It was made clear that Holmes was the dean of the school and that his ideas and decisions would have to be authorized by the Board of Governors.

These dedicated men continued to meet every week through December and the first half of January 1927. The second meeting was held in the offices of Harrison Lewis Company in Beverly Hills. The name of the organization adopted was the "Institute of Religious Science and School of Philosophy". Lewis was directed to lease office space in a building on Wilshire Boulevard in Los Angeles for two years. All memberships would be sold by auction, and the first ten would be known as "charter members".[6]

· 1927 ·

At the January 5, 1927 meeting in the offices of Harrison Lewis Company, a motion was carried that "auction of charter membership be rescinded and stricken from the records,"[7] and the consensus of opinion of the Board of Governors was that "no mention be made of [a] budget until a later date."[8] The Board members were also of the opinion that Clinch, who had been chosen as Toastmaster for the inaugural banquet, should "mention that we need immediately $5,000 in order to take care of initial expenses in the organization work of the Institute of Religious [Science]."[9] Holmes was instructed to arrange for "cards to be distributed on the evening of the banquet . . . to be used for enrollment of charter members," and at the same time for "contribution[s] to the foundation fund."[10] Board member MacDonald suggested that later, "a charter membership certificate be issued to the charter members."[11]

It was the consensus of the Board that "the Institute of Religious Science and School of Philosophy should apply to the State of California for a charter and that that charter should carry provision for a degree of Doctor of Religious Science to be conferred upon its speaker and or leader and other degrees upon its practitioners and teachers."[12]

It was suggested that a provision be made in the constitution for the Board of Governors to serve perpetually. However, it was agreed that that should be worked out later. Armor was appointed acting secretary in the absence of Lewis. The next meeting was set for Wednesday, January 12, 1927, at Brunson's home in Bel Air Estates.[13]

At the January 12 meeting, the "articles of incorporation of the Institute of Religious Science and School of Philosophy were brought before the meeting and read by Ernest Holmes."[14] It was agreed by the Board that the Institute should "be incorporated and thought of as being an institution or school of learning along religious and moral lines, rather than a church."[15] The articles of incorporation were "signed by the five members of the Board of Governors present": Clinch, Brunson, Hathaway, Hendry, and Armor. The signatures of MacDonald and Lewis were to be secured as soon as possible. It was unanimously decided that members of the Board would "defray expenses for an orchestra and minor incidentals at the organization Banquet."[16]

FIRST OFFICIAL MEETING OF THE INSTITUTE, ORGANIZING

At the first official meeting, Holmes was not listed as a trustee:

> Pursuant to written consent of all of the Trustees of the Institute of Religious Science and School of Philosophy[,] a meeting of the Board of Trustees of said Institute of Religious Science and School of Philosophy was held on the 3rd day of March, 1927, at 8 o'clock P.M. at the office of the corporation located at 2511 Wilshire Boulevard in the city of Los Angeles, county of Los Angeles, state of California; Robert L. Hendry, Frank B. Hathaway, Mostyn C. H. Clich [sic], Reginald C. Armor, Lem A. Brunson, J. Farrell McDonald, and Harrison Lewis being present.

. . . Clinch was elected temporary chairman of the Board of Trustees and took his chair as such. . . . Harrison Lewis was elected temporary secretary of the meeting and of the Board of Trustees and assumed the duties of that office.

The temporary chairman then announced that the Certificate of Incorporation of the Institute of Religious Science and School of Philosophy had been duly issued from the office of the Secretary of State of the State of California on February 14, 1927, and that the object of this meeting was to organize the said corporation and the board of trustees thereof by electing all officers, adopting by-laws, and for the transaction of any other business that may be brought before the meeting.

. . . [By unanimously carried motion,] Clinch was elected President of the Board of Trustees and of the corporation and at once assumed the duties of such office.[17]

MacDonald was unanimously elected Vice-President, and Harrison Lewis was elected secretary of the Board and the Corporation; Hathaway was elected treasurer of the Corporation, and Brunson was elected a member of the Executive Committee for the period of one year. Hendry, Brunson, and Armor were chosen as an auction committee in accordance with the bylaws. The secretary (Lewis) was directed to purchase a minutes book, bylaws book, corporate seal, and other such books and materials necessary for the corporation's business function. The Board set the terms of service as follows: Harrison Lewis, one year; Robert Hendry, two years; Frank B. Hathaway, three years; Reginald Armor, four years; Lem Brunson, five years; J. Farrell MacDonald, six years; and Mostyn Clinch, seven years.[18]

Meetings were to be held on the first Wednesday of each month at the Institute headquarters. It was decided that voucher checks were to be used by the Treasurer in payment of accounts, and that a petty-cash account of one hundred dollars was to be established; it was also decided that "officers and prominent members of the Men's Club [would] be invited to meet with the Board at their next regular monthly meeting."[19] The secretary, Lewis, was directed to extend the invitations to the members of the Men's Club, and MacDonald was directed to purchase appropriate parchment embossed with the names of those participating in the endowment fund.[20]

FIRST REGULAR MEETING

The first regular meeting of the Board of Trustees of the new corporation of the Institute of Religious Science and School of Philosophy was held on April 6, 1927. Members of the Men's Club attending were Lewis Wood, a "Mr. Brook," and a "Mr. Fitch."[21]

> The Chairman explained to the members of the Men's Club ... the purposes and aims of the Institute and the reasons for it's [sic] foundation as a University and their hopes for it's [sic] future usefulness and opportunity. . . . [T]he various classes were to be considered as classes in a university and . . . tuition fees paid therefor were to be turned [in to] the Treasurer of the Institute and properly recorded as being received from that source.
>
> Motion was made and carried that the present Men's class automatically be made members of the Men's Club.
>
> The question came up regarding tuition fees for those financially unable to pay and the Chairman appointed a Committee made up of Mr. [Lewis] Wood and Mr. Brook to whom he gave authority to pass special cases where conditions seemed to warrant free tuition. A report of such cases was to be made to the Board of Trustees.[22]

The subject of finding larger quarters for Sunday services was discussed; no decision was made, but the Board intended to keep this matter in mind for the future.[23]

The next regular meeting was held on May 4, 1927. Present were MacDonald, Clinch, Hendry, Hathaway, and Armor. In this meeting was the beginning of many discussions to follow regarding finding necessary funds to carry on the work of the Institute—a subject that was foremost in most of the subsequent meetings.[24]

A MAGAZINE IS BORN

Also raised at the May 4 meeting was the subject of a magazine for the Institute. The Board empowered Holmes to research figures and data for such a publication. There was also discussion of "ways of reporting activity of healing groups."[25] The consensus was "that a testimonial meeting might be held one night a week."[26] This was laid on the table. Holmes was empowered to purchase a fitting gift valued at approximately twenty-five dollars upon the retirement of the current soloist at services to show appreciation for her services.[27]

At the June 1 meeting, a motion was made to change the principal place of doing business to 2511 Wilshire Blvd., Los Angeles, California, and a resolution was passed effecting this change.[28] Holmes was empowered by the Board to "see about membership certificates and order them." He then reported that the magazine costs would be approximately $250 a month, and that $1,500 should be guaranteed for the first two years. The decision of the Board was that the Institute should have a magazine. The Ebell Club was considered as a potential Sunday morning lecture hall, but the cost of space rental was not available at that time. It was decided that a letter stating the aims, needs, and financial condition of the Institute would be placed in the hands of each member.[29]

On July 6, 1927, a letter drafted by Clinch was read to the Board that "gave a résumé of the work of the Institute, in all its aspects."[30] It was agreed that the letter would be mailed to all members, and would be made available on tables at the Institute for anyone interested to take. The idea of a general advisory board was presented, and it was decided that such a board should exist. There was discussion regarding whether to permit advertising in the pages of the magazine. It was decided to leave the question open to the Board "so as to permit certain classes of advertising . . . if so desired."[31] It was also decided that copies of the magazine would sell for 25¢ each, and that the subscription price would be $2.50 per year.[32]

On July 11, 1927, Lewis wrote a letter to the president of the Institute of Religious Science giving his resignation as member and secretary of the Board of Governors. He cited the limited time he had available to serve at this important time in the development of the organization. He said that his many responsibilities would not permit him to take on the additional work of serving on the Board; he ended, "I want all of you to feel that I am with you heart and soul in this great organization which you are so ably perfecting."[33]

At the August 3, 1927 meeting, it was reported that MacDonald had purchased a scroll "upon which is to be inscribed the names of those [members] contributing to the endowment fund."[34] Armor was elected to fill the vacancy of secretary to the Board caused by the resignation of Lewis. It was reported that the Sunday morning auditorium was becoming overcrowded, and Holmes said that within two weeks, he should have information regarding procuring the Ebell Club. He suggested that the Institute handle the sales of all books. The books he authored were to be purchased from him at list price less 25 percent. This arrangement was accepted. A committee of two was assigned to watch for available property to be purchased for the headquarters.[35]

At the September 7 meeting, there were only two motions: first, Armor was authorized to sign checks as secretary of the Board. Second, a lease was executed with the Ebell Club for the use of their theater for Sunday mornings from 10:30 A.M. until 1:00 P.M. for two years, with an additional year's option, at an annual rental of $3,120 to be paid in twelve monthly installments.[36]

At the October 5 meeting, there were several motions made with regard to hiring employees. Josephine Holmes (Ernest's niece, daughter of his brother, Jerome) was to be paid $80 per month beginning September 1 and $100 per month beginning November 1. Augusta Rundel (affectionately known as "Gussie"), a friend and close associate of Holmes, was also to be paid $100 per month beginning September 1. Half of this salary was to be paid from the general fund and half from the magazine account. Additional motions were made to move money from one account to another. Clinch was asked to send several letters, one being to the Ambassador Hotel thanking them for their services and informing them of the move to larger quarters.[37] The amount of $150 was designated to create a sign to be placed each Sunday morning outside the Ebell Club announcing Holmes's lecture, and a letter was also to be sent to each healing group "complimenting and congratulating them on their splendid work."[38]

Several items of business were dealt with at the November 19 meeting worthy of mention. First, an audit and balance sheet to date were requested, with an audit to be performed quarterly after that. An accountant was to be interviewed for this service. Second, Brook resigned as editor of the magazine, and Helen Winton was voted in as his replacement on a trial basis. Two books were authorized to be published, and options were requested for future books by authors Ethel Winton and Helen Van Slyke. The following two motions were made: "It is the sense of the Board of Trustees of this Institute that Mr. Holmes shall at no time appear at any function representing the Institute without the consent of the Board"[39] and "At no time shall any outside speaker appear on the platform of the Institute without first securing the authorization of the Board."[40]

The December 7, 1927 meeting occasioned the decision to create a policy for the Institute's magazine. Armor and MacDonald formed a committee to outline this policy. The subject of broadcasting in the name of the Institute was brought up, with the consensus being that the *Twelve Lessons on the Fundamentals of Religious Science* be broadcast, one lesson each week for twelve consecutive weeks. It was reported that the cost of four radio broadcasts had been arranged for by means of special subscription. The annual salary of Holmes as dean of the Institute of Religious Science was increased as of January 1, 1928 to $10,000 per annum. Holmes was instructed to find an appropriate location for the annual banquet to be held in February 1928. Finally, one hundred practitioner's certificates were authorized to be printed. These certificates were to be given to persons who satisfactorily completed the practitioner's course given by the Institute. The question regarding experience and qualification for the practitioner's certificate was discussed. It was thought that three months of practical experience should apply.[41]

· 1928 ·

The first meeting of 1928 was held on January 4. It was decided that the first official banquet of the Institute would include what was to become an annual meeting with reports on "the various activities of the Institute."[42] It was decided to "amend the by-laws . . . to increase the number of Trustees from seven to nine, the two additional Trustees to be chosen from the members at large and to hold office for . . . one year."[43] Wood was appointed to fill the vacancy in the position of secretary left by Lewis's resignation. It was reported that the legal aspects concerning the issuance of practitioner's certificates were being investigated. Larger office space was needed, so the leasing of additional offices at the headquarters was made for thirteen months for an additional $50 per month.[44]

ERNEST IS ON THE RADIO

A broadcasting agreement was made with radio station KNX (Los Angeles) to broadcast Holmes each Sunday evening from 6:00 to 6:30 P.M. for three months for a rate of $30 per broadcast.

Ethel Winton was approved as permanent editor of the magazine, "subject to the supervision of the Board of Trustees, at a salary of $100 per month."[45] An amendment to the motion stated that she would also receive "a commission of 25 percent of all advertisements written by her except the Institute advertisements."[46] This contract was to run for eight months. The magazine policy committee had decided on the following rates for advertising in the *Religious Science Monthly*: full page, $25 per month; half page, $15 per month; one-third page, $10 per month; and one-sixth page, $5 per month. A 5-percent discount was granted for contracts written for at least a six-month period, and a 10-percent discount for contracts of one year.[47]

BEGINNING YEAR TWO

One year had now passed, and on February 1, 1928, a meeting was again held for the selection of officers. Those voted in place were Clinch as president; MacDonald, vice-president; Armor, secretary; Hathaway, treasurer; and Hendry, Brunson, and Armor, Auditing Committee. The Executive Committee would also include Brunson. These offices were to be held for a period of one year.[48] A Ways and Means Committee was created as a way of supplying supportive membership for the Institute. Holmes, Brunson, and Wood were appointed to a committee to "outline a course of [procedure] for enlisting new members and enlisting their interest in the activities of the Institute."[49] Holmes announced that the graduates of the practitioner's class were forming an alumni association, and a motion was made to endorse the Kiddie Koop Home, a local daycare facility.[50]

Ethel Winton was to take charge of a campaign to increase the magazine subscription. For this, she received a salary of $150 per month plus other expenses. A motion was passed to add two members to the Board, namely Gilbert McElroy and Harold Spear, to fill the nine-member board. Each was added for a one-year term. At the April 11, 1928 meeting, a motion was made to hire a certified accountant to "audit the books of the Institute once a month and render a regular monthly statement."[51]

A discussion was held on the "ways and means of establishing a definite budget for [the maintenance] of the Institute of Religious Science and its various activities."[52] It was suggested that a group of subscribers offer their help in raising this money; the Board intended to "acquire a body of sponsors made up of people vitally interested in the Institute who would subscribe a definite amount."[53] They would meet after the regular Sunday morning lecture, when those wishing to subscribe would be given the opportunity to do so. These invitations would go to those who seriously wanted to support the building itself.

The idea was raised that there should be a closer bond and working relationship between the Board of Trustees and the dean of the Institute. Holmes was directed to get in touch with Christian D. Larson with the idea of contracting with him to give a series of talks during the coming season and determining what Holmes's fee would be.[54]

People were becoming interested in creating individual works under the auspices of the Institute; for this, each group had to be approved by the Institute Board. A Mr. Bryant of San Diego represented one of these groups; however, no action was taken at this meeting. Similarly, there was a discussion about the possibility of creating branch centers of the Institute and their policies of operation, but no decision was reached at this time.[55]

At the April meeting, the subject of the continuation of the radio talks came up again, and it was referred to the Finance Committee. Holmes was instructed to inquire of the radio audience whether they were interested in continuing the broadcasts.

At the May meeting, a report of the sales of the magazine showed a profit in the previous four months (since January 1928), and there had been a decided improvement in subscriptions and counter sales. Larson agreed to present a series of winter classes. It was noted that the primary purpose of both the Men's and Women's Clubs was that of service to the Institute. They were also to be study clubs for the men and women. Holmes reported that interest in the radio audience had proved very satisfying. More than 250 letters had been received emphatically supporting the continuation of his talks in response to the inquiry directed to his audience. The Board authorized up to $1,000 for Holmes to secure teachers for the faculty of the winter classes. He was also instructed to have a catalog designed advertising the winter course of study. He was also given permission to incorporate the Institute Declaration of Principles in a book that he was soon to publish.

At the July 5 meeting, the Board gave full authority to Ethel Winton as editor of the magazine, to accept, reject, and edit all manuscripts presented for publication, subject to the policies of the Institute, with all other associate editors being eliminated.[56]

At the August 1, 1928 meeting, it was decided that "in the final analysis Mr. Holmes should be the one to determine [policy regarding the magazine]."[57] Spear, the business director, suggested that the radio broadcast should be temporarily discontinued as of September 1, 1928. That motion, however, did not carry. It was reported that Ned Chapin, now editor of the magazine, would take over as business manager of the Institute of Religious Science and its publication the *Religious Science Monthly*, at a salary of $400 per month.[58]

In September, the Board was once again on the lookout for a larger facility for the Institute, so floor plans were brought to the September 5 meeting.[59] One building, at the corner of Wilshire and Kingsley, was available for $13,000 annual rental and seemed a suitable space for the headquarters. A building at Hauser and Wilshire was available to rent for $6,000 per year (this address was a considerable distance farther west).[60] At the October meeting, it was decided that the Institute would remain at its present location, paying a monthly rent.[61]

A meeting was held on September 28 in which Armor resigned as secretary. The chairman appointed Chapin to the position until an election could be held for a new secretary.[62] The cost of the radio broadcast, which had been $30 per Sunday, was increased to $40 upon renewal of the year's contract. Monetary gifts were coming in to support the broadcast without funds having to come from the Institute's general fund. It was decided that a contract for one year be entered into with KNX for the Sunday evening broadcast.[63]

After the acceptance of Armor's resignation, Chapin was elected as the new secretary of the Board at the October 3 meeting.[64] Also at this meeting, the Ebell Club Windsor Square Theater was approved by the Board as the Sunday morning lecture hall. The relevant officers were assigned to complete the lease agreement. It was decided that speakers should be cultivated from among Institute personnel who would be capable of speaking for Holmes on the radio when so requested.[65]

A change of the magazine's printer was made at a savings of more than $40 for 2,000 copies. Changes were made at the bank to absorb the magazine account into the Institute account. The monthly magazine report showed $2,751.65 in receipts and $3,360.85 in expenses. The bank balance was approximately $1,880.[66] Other expenses approved at this time included a safe for the office, a filing cabinet, and an adding machine, total expenses for these items not to exceed $200.[67] Monthly salaries as of October 1928 were as follows: Ernest Holmes, $833; Ned Chapin, $400; Augusta Rundel, $125; Josephine Holmes, $125; and May Clark Gosling, $125.[68]

Brunson and Clinch had personally taken an option on a property on Wilshire Blvd. near Norton St., and they were willing to turn the option over to the Institute. This was a vacant lot. After consideration, the Board decided that the lot was too small, so the option was declined, with a thank-you to board members Brunson and Clinch.[69] Holmes was authorized to investigate and act on the possibility of securing Gunsaulus Hall for midweek meetings, with authority to act. A new member, William Haughey, was elected to the Board; he would play a significant role in later years. Policies continued to be created for safer and more efficient business practices. With this in mind, mail would be opened only by Haughey.[70]

During the last meeting of 1928, it was reported that the number of magazine subscriptions had increased by 115 between the mailing of the November magazines and the date of the meeting, December 5.[71]

· 1929 ·

After several resignations from the Board and elections of new members, the officers were Clinch, chairman; Brunson, vice chairman; Hathaway, treasurer; and Chapin, secretary. The Board decided it would create a mailing list by inviting those interested to sign a card, giving their names and addresses. The Board also suggested that "at the appropriate time in the near future, there should be a dinner, at which the question of increasing revenues of the Institute . . . from $15,000 to $20,000 per year should be taken up with the membership."[72] The magazine report showed 860 subscriptions paid in advance and 178 new subscriptions received during December 1928. The first published pamphlet was titled "The Meaning of Religious Science," the main body of which would be from the article of the same title by Holmes in the January 1929 issue of the magazine.[73]

At the meeting of February 6, 1929, there was a discussion of the budget, resulting in a consensus that approximately $50,000 was needed per year. To fund this, it was decided that there should be an active group of some fifty representatives, both men and women, who would work independently— but with explicit direction from the Board—with his or her individual circle of friends with the goal of raising funds to meet budgetary requirements.[74] There was to be a special meeting of the Board on February 10 to further take up this subject.

EXPANSION IDEAS ARE PRESENTED

Two options for a new policy regarding the training of leaders were presented by Holmes:

[First,] that the Institute may be developed as a school of Philosophical training from which persons who had received the training might go out to other cities and start centers for which they would be personally responsible and for which the Institute would have no responsibility. The work in the centers would follow upon the lines of the model work conducted by the Institute in Los Angeles.

Using this plan it was explained there would be no competition with established churches; but rather a tendency for churches to send especially chosen representatives to the Institute for training.

The second plan suggested that the Institute train people and send them out under the auspices of the Institute to establish centers in other localities. Under this plan it was explained the Institute would be responsible for all centers and pay the salary of the center leaders, and would be in direct competition with churches.

Dean Holmes stated in his opinion that the first plan would give the work an infinitely broader scope.[75]

RELIGIOUS SCIENCE MONTHLY SALES CONTINUE TO GROW

The magazine subscriptions and sales continued to grow, and a Mrs. Hillman was given $25 to operate a bookstore, to be open evenings to students and the public.

The popularity of the *Religious Science Monthly* magazine continued to grow. There were now 953 subscribers, with 140 of these new subscriptions from January 1929. In contrast, 1,178 copies were sold at Institute meetings and more than 500 magazines sold on newsstands during the first month of 1929.[76] The Board discussed the policies of the magazine and its name. It was decided that the magazine should be considered "primarily as an aid to the work of the Institute, and as secondary to the work itself."[77] It was decided that the current name of the magazine (*Religious Science Magazine*) be continued and that the policy set forth would be continued for one year. This motion was tabled.[78] [Editor's note: Over the years, the magazine would bring many thousands to the Religious Science movement.]

The cost of a proposed pamphlet, "The Meaning of Religious Science," was quoted at $150 for 5,000 copies and $89 for a second 5,000. A letter was read to the Board from the U.S. Treasury Department stating that the Institute would "not be required to file income tax returns for 1928 [nor for] prior years, nor in the future, as long as there [was] no change in the organization."[79]

A letter from Herbert L. Parker was read suggesting that Sunday morning services be broadcast on the radio and television. Holmes disagreed, asserting that this "would not be in line with the broader policies of the Institute as an Institution of learning."[80] Spear also suggested that applause be discouraged at Sunday morning meetings at the Ebell Club.

An advisory "Committee of Fifteen" submitted a report to the Board in February 1929:

> The report of the Advisory Committee, formed at the suggestion of the Chairman of the Board of Governors, to recommend to the Board ways and means of balancing the budget of the Institute of Religious Science and School of Philosophy for the current year.
>
> On the evening of February 25, 1929, a group of men and women who are interested in the welfare of the Institute of Religious Science and School of Philosophy met at the request of Mr. Chapin to consider certain problems pertaining to the Institute. The meeting was presided over by Mr. Mostyn Clinch, chairman of your Board.

After a brief discussion of the activities of your Board, Mr. Clinch disclosed the fact that the budget of the Institute for the present year was $40,000, while the indicated revenue is but $29,000, thus creating a prospective deficit of $11,000 for the current year.

Your chairman pointed out that as now functioning, the earning power of the Institute has reached its limit, and those present were requested to form an advisory committee for the purpose of devising ways and means of increasing the revenue of the Institute and thus avoiding the prospective deficit.[81]

A MORE DEFINITE ORGANIZATION IS NEEDED

It soon became apparent that in order to expand the organization, its administration could no longer be informal or ambiguous; clear policies and procedures would need to be implemented:

A plan suggested by your chairman [Clinch], together with other plans brought forth by those present, were discussed without arriving at a definite conclusion. . . .

Those agreeing to serve in this capacity [on the Advisory Committee] met . . . and after organizing, proceeded to consider the problem which had been presented to it. . . .

[F]rom the standpoint of organization, the Institute of Religious Science and School of Philosophy is a rather nebulous thing. One member of the committee inquired as to how the Board of Governors is elected, what is their tenure of office, how new members are chosen, etc. No one present could answer all these questions satisfactorily.

Next, the surprising disclosure was brought out that no one present could really claim to be a member of the Institute, since none had ever formally signed any definite membership pledge. Hence, the question naturally arose, if the Institute of Religious Science and School of Philosophy has any members, who are they and how did they join it? And if it has no membership, then just what is the Institute of Religious Science and School of Philosophy?

It was the sense of the committee that it would be rather embarrassing to invite anyone to support an institution that was without definite existence or whose nature could not be described in clear and unmistakable terms.

Another fact which was brought out in unmistakable terms was that, regardless of its name or its ultimate purpose, the Institute of Religious Science and School of Philosophy is essentially a religious institution, a place to which people go to find satisfaction for that soul hunger which is inherent in all normal people; that it is and by its nature must ever continue to be to its supporters a substitute for the church which they, for the most part, left to become associated with it.

Accordingly it was the unanimous judgment of the committee that before the desired purpose; namely, increasing the revenue of the Institute, can be accomplished, a more definite organization is indispensable.

It might be well to state here that there was no disposition on the part of anyone present to underestimate or belittle the importance of the Board of Governors nor to suggest a course that would in any way impair or infringe upon on its powers. On the contrary, the committee is deeply sensible of the invaluable services which the Board has rendered to the Institute and of the supreme importance of its continued directive powers over the affairs of the Institute.

... [W]e unanimously recommend that the following steps be taken:

FIRST. That the religious aspects of the Institute be regarded as paramount, and its educational activities, whatever they may be, as an incidental outgrowth therefrom.

SECOND. That a uniform membership or sponsorship, which shall be open to all interested parties, be created.

THIRD. That in offering memberships or sponsorships, the moral and spiritual benefits to both the individual and the Institute be stressed, while the measure of the financial support stipulated on the sponsorship form be left to the voluntary decision of the applicant.

FOURTH. That the opportunity and importance of becoming formally associated with the Institute be emphasized at the conclusion of the Sunday morning services, at the discretion of Mr. Holmes.

FIFTH. That those seeking sponsorship cards be also supplied with a copy of our statement of faith as set forth in "What we believe and why we believe it," together with an outline of the educational program of the Institute, and that the card be so framed as to indicate an agreement with both the statement of faith and the educational program.

The committee feels that there are hundreds of people whose souls are being satisfied by the Institute as they were never satisfied before, and that those would not only welcome an opportunity to become definitely connected to the Institute but that as a result of such connection they would be actuated toward the Institute by a spirit of loyalty and devotion, as well as a sense of responsibility for the success of the Institute and all that it stands for, which cannot be created by any other means.[82]

THE "COMMITTEE OF FIFTEEN"

On March 6, 1929, the "Committee of Fifteen" was officially established: C. E. Slonaker, Harry Ogg, B. F. Fluno, Guy Chase, J. R. Maxwell, T. A. Dille, Dr. W. Carl Wright, Carroll Loy Stewart, Frank Smith, a Mrs. Hardy, J. A. Goodman, Queen W. Boardman, W. E. Clatworthy, Marian McGuire, and J. P. Horning.

On April 3, 1929, the advisory Committee of Fifteen suggested that the Board pass a resolution authorizing the Committee to establish the "Society of the Institute of Religious Science and School of Philosophy," and issue memberships—called "Fellowships—therein:[83]

It is the sense of this committee that this membership be called a Fellowship, and we hereby suggest that the following application be submitted to prospective members.

"Having read the 'Declaration of Principles' on the back hereof and being heartily in sympathy therewith, I hereby apply for a Fellowship in the Society of The Institute of Religious Science and School of Philosophy.["]

The foregoing is merely our suggestion, and we recommend that your honorable body feel at liberty to change, in any manner which may seem advisable, to the above. Respectfully submitted: Chairman.[84]

After discussion, Brunson's appreciation was extended to the Committee of Fifteen.

CONTINUED CHANGES IN THE ORGANIZATION

At the April 3, 1929 meeting, an amendment to the bylaws was made:

RESOLVED: That the Chairman appoint a Committee of four, two from the Trustees and two from the Advisory Committee, and this committee, together with the attorney for the Institute, to prepare Application for Fellowship in the Institute and also a statement to be printed on the back of the application setting forth in a general way the qualifications and responsibilities of the holders of Fellowship; and be it

FURTHER RESOLVED: That this Resolution [. . .] is hereby notice in writing of a proposed amendment to the bylaws to be considered at the special meeting of the Board of Trustees to be held at 8:00 P.M. on Wednesday, the 8th day of May 1929; these amendments to provide that everyone holding a Fellowship will be entitled to vote at the annual meeting at the Institute for three trustees. One trustee to hold office for seven years and two trustees to hold office for one year each and to amend all provisions in the bylaws which may be inconsistent with this new proviso and expressly including that if graduates of the Institute do not hold Fellowship and are in good standing as such graduates, they be also allowed to vote for Trustees.[85]

At the May 8 meeting, the Board suggested obtaining a mail permit for the cards that were to be returned by those interested in Fellowships. It was also suggested that at this time, the proposed amendment to the bylaws recommended by the Committee of Fifteen not be made, but that it be tabled until everything requiring change to the bylaws was determined.[86]

At the June 9, 1929 meeting, there was a detailed report on the magazine covering subscriptions and other business. It was directed that in the next six issues, a special offer be made to give a year's subscription with a copy of the *Science of Mind* textbook for a total cost of $5. Holmes reported on plans for "The Fundamental Course" to be taught in September and the "Major Course" for six weeks in the fall and three months in the spring. There would be one month's recess during the holidays. The secretary was directed to make arrangements with the Ebell Club for classes to be held Tuesday and Thursday evenings during September at a rental of $100 per night.[87]

At the June 30 meeting, Holmes was empowered to assemble the faculty for the Major Course at the Institute during the coming fall and winter. Holmes was also given the authority to proceed with the organization of the Activities Council. The 1929–30 Bulletin announced the Institute of Religious Science and School of Philosophy's fourth annual Major Course. Courses taught included science, literature, philosophy, religion, psychology, and metaphysics. Several weeks would be devoted to each subject, with Holmes and other instructors teaching these classes.[88]

Radio station KNX reported that the Institute's was the only broadcast that did not try to sell something. It was therefore proposed that a radio Fellowship in the Institute be offered to the public. Holmes suggested that the basis for this fellowship be a series of fifty-two lessons in Religious Science, to be prepared by a special committee; that four of these lessons be published in each issue of the magazine; and that the lessons be offered as an incentive to study by means of radio fellowship.[89]

At the August meeting, it was suggested that one method of raising funds would be for Holmes to ask for money from the platform on Sunday mornings. The objective was $30,000. Those voting against this motion were Brunson and Armor.[90]

NAME CHANGE FOR MAGAZINE PROPOSED

The editor of the magazine recommended that the name be changed to *Science of Mind*. The only member not in favor of this change was a Mr. McReynolds, and the motion was carried. At the October meeting, the secretary was directed to protect the new name by having it registered with the U.S. Patent Office at a cost of $50.[91]

Holmes recommended that the contract with KNX be discontinued at its conclusion on December 30. He suggested that a contract with KEJK, a Beverly Hills station, for one half-hour at 12:00 P.M. every weekday, would cost no more than the amount being paid to KNX. It was directed that the matter be investigated and reported on at the next meeting. On September 11, the committee appointed to investigate the radio stations' rates offers advised that the contract with KNX be renewed for the year beginning October 1, 1929. The motion passed.[92]

A new one-year lease was signed continuing business at 2511 Wilshire Blvd. The Ebell Club lease was also extended for one year. Space at the Ruskin Art Club for the use of the Sunday school was rented for $55 per month from November 1, 1929 to June 30, 1930. A request was made to increase salaries of office staff for a total increase of $65 per month: the director of the healing department from $125 to $150 per month; the bookkeeper, $125 to $135; the secretary to the dean, $125 to $135; the healing department stenographer, $110 to $125; and the book department assistant, $25 to $30. It was decided that no increases in salaries should be considered until after the financial situation had been resolved satisfactorily.[93]

At the January 1930 meeting, it was decided that the Institute should hold midweek testimonial meetings beginning February 1, 1930.

WHAT ELSE WAS HOLMES DOING IN THE 1920S?

During the decade beginning in 1920, besides working to form the Institute of Religious Science and School of Philosophy, Holmes continued his studies, reading, contemplating, meditating, and writing his ideas and thoughts about the Science of Mind and its practical use of the laws of Mind.

He had discontinued traveling the lecture circuit with his brother Fenwicke to remain in Southern California. In 1927, he married Hazel, the woman he would adore for thirty years before her passing in 1957. In 1926, his first major book, *The Science of Mind*, was completed and published by Robert M. McBride of New York. His mother, Anna Holmes, held the copyright. This was the first edition of what has become known simply as "the textbook." All Science of Mind teachings are based on this book. Twelve years later, in 1938, the second edition, edited by Holmes and the editor of the then *Science of Mind* magazine, Maude Allison Lathem, was published; it continues to be used as the primary teaching tool for Science of Mind teachers and students.

RELIGIOUS SCIENCE MONTHLY MAGAZINE

The first issue of *Religious Science Monthly* magazine was published in October 1927.

The price was listed at 25¢, or $2.50 for the year. The front cover reads: "A magazine of Christian Philosophy" and references an article, "Visualization" by Ernest S. Holmes. On the inside cover: "Institute of Religious Science and School of Philosophy"; "A Nonsectarian College of Metaphysics"; "Ernest S. Holmes, Founder"; "Incorporated under the laws of the State of California; 2511 Wilshire Boulevard, Los Angeles, California"; and the phone number, "WAshington 7909", as well as the following statement:

Object of the Institute:

Primarily, it is an institution of learning that in no way competes with any established church or doctrine, existing solely for the purpose of enlightenment on Religious Science and its application to the greatest of all Arts—that of Life itself.

For those who wish a scientifically deduced course of mental training undivorced from the highest concept of Truth; for those who desire honesty, intelligence, freedom from any and all sense of mystery, and above all else, practicability, in their understanding of Unity, this school has been founded. Offering, as it does, a course in the Science of Mind and Religion so comprehensive in its scope that its appeal is general, teachers, practitioners, specialists along these lines and those who desire to remold their own understanding as an aid toward greater harmony of individual expression, will all find herein unique opportunities for guidance.

Directors: Mostyn C. H. Clinch, Chairman; Frank B. Hathaway, Lem A. Brunson, J. Farrell MacDonald, Robert L. Hendry, Reginald C. Armor.[94]

Meditation for Saturday, October 1, 1927:

ALL Wisdom and Knowledge is from within, and my God, who is All-Knowing, is also within.[95]

Meditation for Sunday, October 2, 1927:

I am at peace and rest in the knowledge of the All-Good which is ever at hand.[96]

The contents include an article called "Reflections" (J. Farrell MacDonald), "At-one-ment" (Helen Van Slyke), "The Theory of Visualization" (Ernest S. Holmes), "A Treatment" (Marie Deal), "The Right and the Wrong of It" (Ethel Winton), "The Relation of the Individual to the Universal Mind" (Clarence Mayer), "Everywoman's Club," "The Message of Self-Expression" (Emily G. Marshall), "Announcement" (Ernest S. Holmes), "A Men's Club with a Purpose" (Ned L. Chapin), "Questions and Answers," "Junior Department" (Mabel A. Langdon), "Dorothy Doubts Adventure" (Ethel Winton), "One Lamp Lights Another" (C. Warren Temple), "Announcing a Complete Course in the Science of Mind," "The Oak and the Leaves" poem (Helen Van Slyke), "Happiness" (Alberta Smith), "Practitioners," and "Book Department."[97]

Included was an "Announcement" by Ernest S. Holmes:

The Institute of Religious Science and School of Philosophy of Los Angeles, California, in publishing Religious Science—a magazine of Christian Philosophy—does not enter a competitive field; for it will not discuss current events, either local, national, or international; it will not produce fiction or make any attempt at research in the field of physical-science.

The purpose of this magazine will be to instruct ethically, morally, and religiously, from a scientific viewpoint of life and its meaning.

A semi-religious periodical, ethical in its tendency, moral in its tone, philosophical in its viewpoint, it will seek to promote that universal consciousness of life which binds all together in one great Whole. It is to be tolerant, charitable, and kindly in its aspect. The world needs such a periodical and it will find its place in the mind and hearts of thousands who are looking for a greater realization of life, peace, poise, and happiness. It will also be the purpose of Religious Science to present to its readers a systematic and comprehensive study of the subtle powers of mind and spirit, in so far as they are now known; and to show how such powers may be consciously used for the betterment of the individual and the [human] race.

The [human] race is entering a new era—no one who observes can doubt this; and this new age will seek, and is already seeking, to make practical use of its entire knowledge, whether it be ethical, religious, scientific, moral, or philosophical. All truths lead back to one central theme, namely, man and his relationship to the universe in which he lives. It is to be the purpose of this periodical to show that this relationship is real, direct, and dynamic; that there is such a thing as Truth and that it may be known in a degree sufficient to enable the one knowing, to live a happy and useful life, wholesome, healthful, and constructive; to engage in all the activities of life without being depressed by them, and to feel certain that his future is in the hands of an eternal Power and Goodness and that nothing real can ever cease to be.

Those wishing further information regarding this course, which is given but once each year, should write to The Institute of Religious Science, 2511 Wilshire Boulevard, Los Angeles,

California. Upon request, either by letter or personal inquiry, a complete synopsis of the course will be given to all who are interested.[98]

On the next-to-last page, the meditation for Sunday, October 30, 1927:

I am at One with the All Good for my life is the Life of God within me.[99]

On the next-to-last page is also the list of practitioners, many of whom had offices in the Institute: Marie Deal, Alberta Smith, Clarence Mayer, Emily G. Marshall, and Anna Holmes. Cora J. Bamford, Ada Seymour, and Maye Taylor had offices in their homes.[100]

The "Our Book Department" page lists six books by Ernest Holmes, five by Fenwicke Holmes, and six by Thomas Troward. It tells how to order them. There is an advertisement for Clinch & Thurtle Realtors.[101]

On the inside of the back cover is "What We Believe," slightly different from the one given in recent years, and stated in first person, "I believe . . ." [Editor's note: The masculine neutral pronoun (man, men, etc.) was common usage at that time.]

What We Believe

I believe in God the Living Spirit Almighty; One, Indestructible, Absolute and Self-Existent Cause. This One manifests Itself in and through all creation but is not absorbed by Its creation. The manifest universe is the body of God. It is the logical and necessary outcome of the infinite self-knowingness of God.

I believe in the incarnation of the Spirit in man and that all men are incarnations of the One Spirit.

I believe in the eternity, the immortality and the continuity of the individual soul forever and ever expanding.

I believe that the Kingdom of Heaven is within myself and that I experience this Kingdom to the degree that I become conscious of it.

I believe the ultimate goal of life to be a complete emancipation from all discord of every nature, and that this goal is sure to be attained by all.

I believe in the unity of all life, that the Highest God and the [innermost] God is one God.

I believe that God is personal to all who feel this Indwelling Presence.

I believe in the direct revelation of Truth through the intuitive and spiritual nature of man, and that any man may become a revelator of Truth who lives in close contact with the Indwelling God.

I believe that the universal Spirit, which is God, operates through a Universal Mind, which is the Law of God; and that I am surrounded by this Creative Mind which receives the direct impress of my thought and acts upon it.

I believe in the healing of the sick through the power of this mind.

I believe in the control of conditions through the power of this Mind.

I believe in the Eternal Goodness, the Eternal Loving-Kindness and the Eternal Givingness of Life to all.

I believe in my own soul, my own spirit and my own destiny, for I understand that the life of man is God.[102]

BOOKS PUBLISHED BEFORE OR DURING THE 1920S

Creative Mind (1919); *Creative Mind and Success* (1919); *The Science of Mind* (1926); *Meditations for Self Help and Healing* (1926); *Immortality* (1927); *What We Believe* (1927, first printed in Science of Mind magazine); *The Bible in the Light of Religious Science* (1929).

3

The 1930s:
The Development of the
Institute Continues

You are important to life. That which created you and brought you this far will take care of you the rest of eternity. You are a citizen of the universe, and no claim that you can make is too much for the Power which is within you to accomplish. It knows no limitations, not even the ones you have placed in your own thinking. Give this Power great works to do by maintaining great ideas in your consciousness. The creative process in your subconscious mind is inexhaustible. It knows neither worry nor fatigue. It is perfect in its precision. Give it great goals to accomplish. Use it for greatness.

Raymond Charles Barker, *The Power of Decision*[1]

A realization of the Presence of God is the most powerful healing agency known to the mind of man.

Ernest Holmes, *The Science of Mind*[2]

· 1930 ·

The decade of the 1930s began with a new magazine, in name and appearance. Remember, this was during the Great Depression. Obviously, such words meant nothing to Ernest Holmes. Thousands came to hear him speak on mental treatment and healing of their lives.

There was a great and growing interest in his radio program, and many wanted to know more about what he called "mental treatment." A brochure was created to send to those who requested it: "Mental Treatment for Healing and Prosperity." Magazine revenues were steadily increasing, as well as subscriptions and newsstand sales. In March 1930, the total magazine distribution increased to over 7,000.

THE MAGAZINE CHANGES ITS NAME TO SCIENCE OF MIND

As of January 1930, the name of the magazine was changed to *Science of Mind*. The cover of the January issue reads:

> In this issue
>
> The Meaning of Religious Science
>
> by Ernest S. Holmes
>
> The Importance of the Imagination
>
> by Willett L. Hardin
>
> The Discipline of the Mind
>
> by Ameen U. Fareed
>
> Daily Meditations – page 36
>
> 25¢ per copy; $2.50 for year[3]

The inside cover gives the contents: "A New Year's Suggestion" (H. [Hazel] Foster Holmes), "Editorial," "The Meaning of Religious Science" (Ernest S. Holmes), "Figures on a Dial" (Harry Earnshaw), "The Importance of the Imagination" (Willett L. Hardin), "Behind the Symbol" (Katherine Lipke), "The Discipline of the Mind" (Ameen U. Fareed), "What's Behind it All?" (Allan M. Wilson), "The Science of Mind (The New Birth—Conscious Use of the Law of Creation—Definite Work and Healing)" (Ernest S. Holmes), "Daily Readings," "Daily Meditations," "Building the Child's Mind" (Christian D. Larson), "I Am Resolved" (poem by Helen Van Slyke), and "Practitioner's Roster."[4]

The inside cover also reads:

The Science of Mind Magazine is published monthly by the Institute of Religious Science and School of Philosophy, Inc., 2511 Wilshire Boulevard, Los Angeles, California

Entered as second class matter November 13th, 1928, at the Postoffice [sic] at Los Angeles, California, under the act of March 3, 1879.

Subscribers' copies are mailed to reach them on the 20th of each month preceding the date of issue. If you do not receive your copy promptly, please report at once.

Subscription price is $2.50 per year. Single copies 25c. . . .

Sample copies will be mailed to any address free of charge.

The Science of Mind Magazine is on sale in Seattle at Seattle Truth Center, suite 327, Hotel Gowman; in San Francisco at the Metaphysical Library, 177 Post Street; in London, England at 9 Percy Street and 93 Mortimer Street; at various Truth Centers in the western states and on news stands throughout Southern California.[5]

On page 1 appears the following:

A New Year Suggestion

H. Foster Holmes

Try this daily dozen;—turn on the wheel of intelligence until they become a habit:

TOLERANCE
CHEERFULNESS
FORTITUDE
LOYALTY
OPTIMISM
ENTHUSIASM
CONSIDERATION
SINCERITY
EFFICIENCY
GRATITUDE

TENACITY

MAGNANIMITY

Those who have used this treatment recommend it. To obtain the best results practice at home.[6]

The "Book List" includes a booklet by Ernest Holmes and seven of his books, including *The Science of Mind* and *The Bible in the Light of Religious Science*. Also listed are seven books by Thomas Troward, one by Helen Van Slyke, *Essays* by Ralph Waldo Emerson, one book by Ernest Trattner, four books by Fenwicke Holmes, one by Allan M. Wilson, two by James Allen, twenty-six books by Christian D. Larson, and four miscellaneous brochures listed variously at 50¢ and $1.00 each.[7]

On the back cover, we find an affirmation: "I AM kindness and good will toward all men. This is the best year I have ever lived."[8]

RAISING FUNDS CONTINUES AS A PRIORITY

There was a "$10 and Up Club" created to raise funds for the continued increase in costs of the Institute. A young people's group was suggested: "It is recognized that the children's Sunday school is very important and that everything possible should be done to develop this work."[9] The hiring of a secretary for Holmes was considered. In the Healing Department, the number of request letters was growing steadily, with almost three hundred per week. There had been up to a hundred people meeting with this department. The financial campaigns were ongoing, and there continued to be a deficit.[10]

At the June 1930 meeting, it was reported that the magazine sales continued to grow. For the month of July 1930, total distribution was up to 8,750 issues. A committee was created "to outline a definite policy with regard to the Hollywood Branch of the Institute and to other Branches that might be established."[11]

GREATER ACKNOWLEDGMENT OF ERNEST HOLMES'S WORK IS REQUESTED

A letter from Harrison Lewis to the president of the board, Mostyn Clinch, stated:

I believe that the time has come when we should create, in the Institution of Religious Science, the office of "Doctor of Religious Science," which degree should be awarded according to the authority vested in us by the State of California.

This degree should be conferred upon Ernest Holmes in acknowledgment of the great service that he has rendered in the field of Religious Science.

I wish you would take this up with the members of the Board of Directors of the Institute of Religious Science, and arrange to bring about this much deserved act, to show our appreciation of the inspiration and invaluable service which Ernest Holmes has afforded this generation.[12]

RADIO BROADCAST ENDS FOR THE PRESENT TIME

At the October 8, 1930 meeting, it was decided that the radio broadcast—which had been discontinued as of October 1—would not be renewed at that time. It was agreed that this had been the appropriate action to take.[13] Because of the continued shortage of funds, Holmes presented his plans for courses relative to reducing the overhead of the Institute by paying no salaries and hiring special lecturers as needed. The board terminated all contracts with lecturers effective April 1, 1931.[14]

December 1, 1930 brought a drop in the rental fee for the Ebell Club to $75, from the $80 that had been paid in 1930. At the December 18 meeting, a loan of $3,000 from the bank was authorized "for the purpose of paying current bills now past due."[15]

1930 QUARTERLY JOURNAL PUBLICATION

The first issue of the *Quarterly Journal of Science, Religion, and Philosophy* included the following items:

Foreword—Dr. Willett L. Hardin

The Institute of Religious Science and School of Philosophy— Ernest Holmes, Dean

What Has Happened to Our Religion?—Dr. John G. Hill

The Conquest of Nature and Its Influence on Mankind—Dr. Willett L. Hardin

Religion and New Thought—Dr. William L. Barth

Driving Power of the Emotions—Dr. Ameen U. Fareed

Natural versus Civil Laws—Dr. Frederick Leonard

Moody's "The Faith Healer"—Katharine Merrill

The Law of Increase—Christian D. Larson.[16]

1931 QUARTERLY JOURNAL PUBLICATION

The *Quarterly Journal* Volume 2, Number 3 is the first full edition on file. The cover reads:

Quarterly Journal, Science, Religion, Philosophy, edited by Willett L. Hardin, Ph.D.

Published by the Science-Religion-Philosophy Publishing Company Ltd., Los Angeles, California.[17]

The Autumn 1931 issue price was 50¢. The inside cover gives the address of Science-Religion-Philosophy, 2511 Wilshire Blvd., Los Angeles, California (the same as the Institute's address). The "Contributors to Symposium on Immortality" are listed:

Honorable Martin Wade, Judge of District Court, Iowa; Edwin H. Lewis, Dean, Lewis Institute, Chicago, Illinois; Rev. William L. Barth, formerly Congregational Minister, Student of Comparative Religions; Rev. A. D. Stauffacher, Minister, Claremont Church, Claremont, California; Ernest Holmes, Dean, Institute of Religious Science and School of Philosophy, Los Angeles; Carl F. Knopf, PhD, Professor of Hebrew History and Archeology, University of Southern California; Ameen U. Fareed, M.D., Physician and Psychologist; Honorable Thomas G. Patten, formerly U. S. Congressman and Postmaster of New York City; Rev. B. G. Carpenter, Throop Memorial Church, Pasadena, California; Ernest R. Trattner, Jewish Rabbi; John G. Hill, Director of Religious Education, University of Southern California; Christian D. Larson, writer of inspirational and metaphysical subjects; Willett L. Hardin, formerly Lecturer on Physical Chemistry at the University of Pennsylvania; and John H. Shedd, Professor of Physics, Occidental College.[18]

On page 1 is found the following information:

Editor is Willett L. Hardin, Ph.D.; Ernest Holmes – Carl F. Knopf, Ph.D., Associate Editors; Lem A. Brunson, Business Manager. All rights reserved. Autumn, October 1931. Subscription price $2.00 per year. Published by the Science-Religion-Philosophy Publishing Company, 2511 Wilshire Blvd., Los Angeles, California. Advertisement for Symposium on Reason and Religion, Trends in Religious Movements, Scientific Discoveries, Einstein and Relativity, Relation and the Natural Sciences and Social Sciences.

Back cover:

This symposium on immortality of fourteen contributors specially prepared by the Quarterly Journal of Science Religion Philosophy as a gift edition.

There is a premium offer for the year 1930 of a bound library volume given free while they last for a three-year subscription to one address, or for three one-year subscriptions to three separate addresses. This is a bound copy of *Quarterly Journal* for the four quarters of 1930.[19]

· 1931 ·

MEETING REGARDING THE QUARTERLY JOURNAL

In the March 11, 1931 meeting, the following was reported:

Trustee Holmes reports that as of March 11, 1931, the Quarterly Journal has now been definitely taken over by the University of Southern California and that the Institute will waive all claims to same but agrees to take one thousand copies a month for the first year. They will be sold at a figure making it possible for the Institute to retail them for twenty-five cents per copy.

Mr. Holmes brought up the subject of the indebtedness to the Science, Religion, Philosophy Publishing Company and to the form of a note upon which the Institute would pay regular banking interest stating that he felt it only a legitimate and fair thing to do in token of good faith since the Institute was not now able nor would likely be able during the summer to pay the Science, Religion, Philosophy Publishing Company any appreciable amount for the indebtedness incurred by that company in taking over the business of the magazine.

Trustee Holmes further reports that the ownership of the Science of Mind magazine comes back to the Institute with the July issue stating that this would mean the assuming of approximately sixteen hundred unfulfilled subscriptions which would cancel the $840.00 obligation of the Institute to that company. Trustee Holmes stated that it was his feeling that advertising should not be carried by the magazine since same did not pay for itself. Trustee Wunder moved that the Institute take the magazine over, business of which to be run as a separate department within the Institute with its own bank account, and that Mr. Chambers be made both the Treasurer and the Business Manager of same. The motion was seconded by Armor, passed.[20]

A ninety-day note was signed for $2,750 at 7 percent interest for publication of the magazine.

THE WILTERN THEATER IS ON THE HORIZON

For quite some time, Holmes had been watching the construction of the Wiltern Theater, inquiring as to its completion and the possibility of rental for his Sunday morning lectures. In September 1931, the building was completed.

At this time, Clinton Wunder expressed a desire to be invited to join the Institute as an employee. $10,000 had to be raised in order to hire him. He was associated with the Academy of Motion Picture Arts and Sciences, and his expertise and connections were considered valuable. Further, it was thought that he could be helpful in securing rental of the Wiltern, owing to his access to the theater's owner. At the October 1931 meeting, a motion was made to designate Holmes lifetime dean of the Institute and to hire Wunder as co-dean. A letter went to Wunder from W. W. Haughey, currently chairman of the Board, offering him the position at $10,000 per year. "Mr. Ernest Holmes suggested to the Board that you [Clinton Wunder] be invited to join the organization," the letter read in part, "to share with him in the direction and management of the activities of this Institute. . . . We believe the proposed combined leadership of Mr. Holmes and yourself will make it possible for us to enter successfully that era of expansion and development for which the Institute is now ready."[21]

At the November 13, 1931 meeting, a letter from Rabbi Julius Leibert of Temple Emanu-El was read stating the terms under which the Institute would take occupancy of the temple for its Sunday services, and speaking of the advantages to the two groups: "Our philosophy is based on the unity of good, the oneness of all life," Haughey wrote. "It is not different from but identical with yours, and we trust that the drawing together of our two movements, partly under one roof, will prove of mutual benefit..."[22] Holmes further reported on this, saying that he felt that by having a morning and evening service on Sundays, the accommodations at Temple Emanu-El would be much greater than those at the Ebell Club.

Additionally, there was to be a reception and dinner dance to honor Dr. and Mrs. Wunder, plans to be made by the Women's Service and Social Club, and a letter was written to Lem Brunson thanking him for his "generosity in taking care of the payment of two hundred and fifty dollars . . . on the Institute note to the Security Bank."[23]

The 1932 budget for the Institute shows the amount required to operate the Institute in 1932 and pay off all old accounts due totaled $63,966. Of that, $30,000 was for salaries and $6,446 for accounts payable past due. The estimated income from book sales, contributions, Sunday offerings ($10,000), miscellaneous, and so forth was $29,600. This left a sum of $34,366 to be raised by special contributions.[24]

· 1932 ·

At the May 12, 1932 meeting, a request was made to ban petitions

Trustee Holmes expressed himself as desiring that the Board should pass a resolution that no petitions of any nature whatever should be placed in the Institute meetings or rooms for signatures and that the Institute should never in any way, as an organization, sponsor the candidacy of any individual for any office. Motion seconded by Trustee Wunder, with the suggestion that notice of said resolution be carried in the monthly Calendar of activities. Motion was carried.[25]

· 1935 ·

PURCHASE OF NEW PROPERTY

There was discussion of a property located at 3251 West 6th Street, Los Angeles, California. The need of necessary funds for its purchase was noted, June 15 being the date by which option on the property must be taken up.

This was the site of the Holtzclaw Building, whose unusual beauty and charm served only to complement the premier interior-design firm of the same name doing business there.

Once the building had been purchased, Holmes and Armor, along with Gussie Rundel, strolled through the building and made their choices of offices. Upon passing the portico of three arches and entering the large foyer on 6th Street, one confronted straight ahead a long, wide hallway off of which was a series of rooms decorated in different period styles. These had been the firm's showrooms. Armor chose a rather small office on the right, next to the proposed bookstore. It had beautiful wood paneling and a marble fireplace; its window faced New Hampshire Street. At the end of the hall was a large office that Holmes chose as an appropriate space, and just outside of the office was plenty of room for his secretary and other clerical help. Also at the end of the hall, on the right, was the office chosen for Hazel Holmes. Hazel, the adored wife of Ernest and a much-celebrated practitioner in her own right, would see clients here.

The rooms along the hall were used by practitioners, who would see clients during the week. There were also rooms for a library, a chapel, and upstairs, an auditorium for classes. Downstairs was a large room with a kitchen as well for the accounting offices, clothing donations, and young-adult Wednesday-night meetings. This was the Fiesta Room. Upstairs, there was a large auditorium where speakers, such as Holmes, Armor, and other ministers would give lessons to the young people. After the lecture, they would go downstairs to the Fiesta Room for dancing, refreshments, table tennis, and other socializing. [Note: At the end of this chapter, you will find a complete description of the Institute building.]

· 1936 ·

Throughout 1936, the Institute continued to settle into its new building and develop its activities. On February 11, 1936, there was discussion regarding the beautiful and rare tapestry that was presented to the Institute by Mr. and Mrs. Ernest DuPont. The Board stated its wish that Mr. and Mrs. DuPont be formally acknowledged by the Board. The Secretary was instructed to write a letter to Mr. and Mrs. DuPont thanking them for their compliment and generosity paid the Institute by presentation of the tapestry.[26] On September 13, 1936, it was recorded that a payment of $200 was made to Fenwicke Holmes for his Sunday morning talks during the month of August 1936.[27] On October 13, 1936, Mr. and Mrs. Haughey gave a gift to the Institute of a flag, which was received with thanks and appreciation. The flag would be on the platform at every meeting at the Wiltern Theater.[28]

On behalf of the Institute, Holmes reported that he had "contracted to broadcast over radio station KFAC for three fifteen minute periods each week ... the cost of this activity would amount to $35 a week and ... individuals were subscribing the money; a large part had been paid and subscribed already."[29] Evidently, work that Pacific Electric was doing near the building in moving earth and using fill caused flooding in the basement of the Institute. Pacific Electric agreed to pay $500 toward repairing the floor damaged by the flooding. For the summer session (August), Fenwicke Holmes was to be hired as the speaker.[30]

On April 18, 1939, a building-fund unit issue was authorized. A committee made up of Haughey, Holmes, and Powers was authorized to make application to the State Corporation Commission for a permit to issue $100,000 worth of building-fund units bearing 5 percent interest, to be issued in accordance with Commission rules; and that upon receipt of the permit, the officers of the Institute be authorized to offer these building-fund units for sale.[31]

On May 16, 1939, the chapter organization plan and bylaws were adopted. These set forth the requirements for group affiliation as a chapter of the organization—the Religious Science Chapter Association.[32]

In the January 1927 issue of *Religious Science Monthly*, there had been eight practitioners listed. In the January 1930 issue, now named *The Science of Mind* magazine, thirty practitioners were listed.

DESCRIPTION OF THE INSTITUTE OF THE CHURCH OF RELIGIOUS SCIENCE

The following is a description of the Institute of the Church of Religious Science, located in the Holtzclaw Building at 3251 West 6th Street, Los Angeles, California, as described by Mr. Bill Lynn, business manager of the church, in 1970.

The building was built in 1920 by the nationally known architect Mr. [John B.] Holtzclaw. He was considered to be the best in Los Angeles.

The building is of Italian design, and an effort has been made to keep the original concept. There are three floors overall.

As you enter the front door, you are impressed by the hand-wrought iron grill-work on the massive door.

Coming into the lobby, you see a very large and stately room with hand-carved, hand-decorated beamed ceiling. From this vaulted roof hang two magnificent imported Venetian glass chandeliers.

The size of the room is increased by two recessed windows. They are furnished by an old monk's table, and ancient chest and chairs.

The very old antique credenza under the leaded-glass window and running its full length, was a gift of Queenie Boardman. This beautiful window lends a soft benign light over all.

The large fireplace was designed by Stanford White. It is flanked by a pair of Savonarola chairs, and above it hangs a fifteenth-century triptych of unusual interest. On each side of the fireplace hang fifteenth-century velvet brocades woven for a ducal palace. These are one of three pairs given by Doris Kenyon to Dr. Holmes for this building, along with many other precious antiques. The three pairs of brocades were purchased by her husband, the late Milton Sills, a personal friend of Dr. Holmes, who paid $20,000 for them.

A large antique escritoire, with secret drawers that breathe of mystery, is most interesting.

The imported Italian carpet, a soft muted red, was woven in Italy especially for this room. After more than thirty years, it is still as colorful and softly shaded as ever.

Doris Kenyon brought her interior decorator with her when the gift was made, and he said there was not another place in the world used as a school as nicely furnished as this one.

A bronze statue called Gloria Victis, with fine carved pedestal, is of special interest. It depicts the Valkyrie carrying the wounded soldier to Valhalla. This statue is valued at $6,000.

From the lobby you enter the long spacious hall through an impressive imported arched doorway. On the wall, on each side of the hall or concourse, are hung many pictures. Among these is a lifelike and truly excellent painting of Dr. Holmes, done by the late Ferdinand Earle, one of the finest portrait artists.

COMMENTARY BY BILL LYNN AT A FUNCTION IN 1970

Before starting descriptive commentary, tell about the plans in store . . . not dreams . . . for Religious Science has no room for the dream world . . . but definite plans which we know are coming to pass, and the groundwork is being laid right now . . . the large parking area, the Institute building and the Youth Center—all will be razed to be replaced by a fifty-two-story skyscraper with four levels of underground parking . . . this to house the Institute of Religious Science—a fast-growing organization meeting the needs of mankind today—1970, and tomorrow. A center where, it may be said, "Religion and Science met, studied and taught." The name of the game in this day and age is "manpower"—trained in this modern skyscraper to carry on the work—the philosophy of Religious Science throughout the world.

Now . . . back to the Institute building . . . formerly the display rooms and work shop of interior decorators . . . built in 1920 by the nationally known architect Mr. [John B.] Holtzclaw and purchased by the Institute of Religious Science in 1935 with very little money, but with mountains of faith and confidence built on the solid basis of tested treatment. The offices were moved from the 2511 Wilshire Blvd. second-floor rented quarters . . .

In the foyer . . . note the hand-wrought iron grill work, sixteenth century—highly valued as a work of art and very rarely does one see work to compare to it in this or any other country . . . the tapestry over the entrance—seventeenth-century Flemish—a gift from the DuPont family to Dr. Holmes . . . to the right of the fireplace, the bronze statue, Gloria Victus, is a fine work in bronze by Mercie and depicts angels carrying the body of the soldier to Valhalla . . . or Heaven . . . the two large lanterns, one at each side of the entrance, are old reproductions of the fifteenth-century Spanish Renaissance period . . . The drapery hangings each side of the fireplace, donated by the late move star, Doris Kenyon—wife of Milton Sills—are fifteenth-century Italian . . . the lantern behind me, on the staircase, is an excellent reproduction of sixteenth-century Italian work; the top of the lantern revolves, and one of the side panels is hinged to become a door . . . on the east wall is an antique credenza—original sixteenth-century Spanish . . . candlesticks on the credenza are sixteenth-century Spanish, also—consider, if you will, that this furniture was of the same period as Columbus . . . The fireplace—a work of art designed by the famous Stanford White . . . the two chandeliers above are Venetian hand-blown glass, made especially for this building . . . the north wall cabinet is seventeenth-century Spanish Renaissance.

We continue into the Galleria; on the west wall as you enter next to room number twelve . . . a restored painting by Italian painter (Verona) Paolo Cagliari (1528–88), Susanna and the Elders . . . above entrance to Galleria is a lacquered color lithograph entitled Hope from the painting by James Watts in the London Gallery . . . oil painting of Dr. Holmes on the east wall by Ferdinand Earle, done in 1948 . . . across the room and above the clock, a very good copy of Rembrandt's Mother . . . in Dr. Reginald Armor's office take special note of the imported wood paneling on walls and the ornate irreplaceable drapery fixtures . . . Dr. Ballentine Henley's office (number five) . . . note the painted door—all doors imported and unfortunately most were painted over the beautiful artwork covered . . . at the north end of the Galleria and against the wall, priceless prie-dieu, purchased in Vatican City and presented to Ernest Holmes by Milton Sills—fifteenth-century . . . Dr. Holmes's office, now being used by Dr. Gifford, tapestries seventeenth-century Flemish . . . cabinet, Jacobean origin (after James I of England), seventeenth-century . . . staff work (composition of plaster and hemp fiber cast in molds and wired or nailed) imported . . . painting of Dr. Holmes, 1938 . . . ceiling imported from Europe in one piece . . . this entire room will be moved as it now stands to the new high-rise quarters. . . .

BOOKS PUBLISHED DURING THE 1930S

Books and booklets by Ernest Holmes published in the 1930s: *Values*, with M. Sills (1932); *Fore-gleams of Eternal Life*; *Religious Science Fundamentals*; *Mind Healing*; *The Ebell Lectures on Spiritual Science* (1934); *It's Up to You* (1936); *Questions and Answers on the Science of Mind with Alberta Smith* (1935); and *The Science of Mind*, second edition, revised and enlarged (1938); *Religious Science* (booklet, 1932).

4

The 1940s:
World Turbulence and
Institute Changes

'Thy kingdom come, Thy will be done on earth as it is in heaven' is a
recognition of the unity which takes place when the real is linked to
the ideal. It is then that experience becomes a legitimate offspring,
in the outer world, of inner states of happiness and well-being.

Ernest Holmes, *The Ebell Lectures*[1]

In 1940, Europe was in the middle of World War II, with the possibility of the United States taking part soon. What did this mean to Ernest Holmes and the Institute of Religious Science?

· 1941 ·

PEACE RALLY WITH FRANK H. ROBINSON

In September 1941, Holmes, together with Dr. Frank H. Robinson, held a peace rally in the Philharmonic Auditorium in Los Angeles. The headline read: "Let there be immediate peace on earth through the power of the living God." This was the largest auditorium in the Los Angeles area, and it was filled to capacity.[2]

At the September 16, 1941 meeting, there was a discussion regarding the Holmes–Robinson peace meetings.

Holmes reported that he "had arranged with Dr. Robinson, Founder of Psychiana™, to conduct a series of open meetings at the Philharmonic Auditorium, in the interest of World Peace; both he and Robinson acting as individuals and not as representatives of any organization, not selling or giving away literature. [Holmes] stated, further, that there was a possibility of making an arrangement with Dr. Robinson whereby he would solicit his graduate students of "Psychiana" to take the Institute's Extension Course as advanced work."

A brief discussion followed, in which the Board members expressed their interest in and approval of such an arrangement.[3]

On October 2, the ordination of Dr. Frank Robinson was recognized. The Committee on Education recognized Robinson's previous ordination as a Baptist minister and requested that he be recognized by the Institute.[4]

A special meeting was called on October 14, 1941, before the regular meeting on October 17, to discuss the "American Spiritual Awakening." The president "called on Trustee Holmes to outline the aims of the movement, and the method to be employed in their accomplishment. A discussion followed, in which individual members of the Board expressed their opinions as to the advisability of such an understanding, but action on the matter was postponed until the next meeting."[5]

At the regular board meeting on October 17, the discussion of October 14 continued regarding the "American Spiritual Awakening" organization:

Trustee Holmes stated that both he and Dr. Robinson believed in the possibility of such a movement accomplishing a definite spiritual awakening throughout the country; that Dr. Robinson was well equipped in his plant in Moscow, Idaho to handle the campaign through the mails (which, in his opinion[,] was the only way it could be handled satisfactorily); and such part as the Institute might take in this movement would in no sense bring criticism or lack of prestige. He stated further that he had conferred in length with Dr. Robinson, with reference to his soliciting his graduate students to purchase the Institute's Extension Course and the Science of Mind magazine; that Dr. Robinson was amenable to this, and for this reason he would like to show the good faith of the Institute by going ahead with Dr. Robinson in furthering the American Spiritual Awakening movement for at least a trial period of three months.

A discussion followed in which each individual member of the Board expressed his opinion.[6]

After much discussion and a negative vote of several of the board members,

> Trustee Holmes stated that in view of the amount of opposition from members of the Board, who had given the matter sincere and intelligent thought, he did not feel that he wished to continue to take part in the movement. He suggested that if it was agreeable to the Board, he would contact Dr. Robinson, explaining that the Institute wishes to withdraw from the American Spiritual Awakening, but desires to make an arrangement with him whereby he would advertise our Course and magazine on a purely business basis, but without any affiliation between the Institute and Psychiana. The Board expressed unanimous approval of such an effort.[7]

At the November 18, 1941 meeting, Holmes reported that "the Institute is taking no part whatsoever in this movement; that all mail connected with the movement which comes to the Institute is being forwarded, unopened, to Dr. Frank Robinson at Moscow, Idaho, and that Dr. Robinson is continuing to conduct a mail campaign in behalf of the movement, but without any assistance from the Institute."[8]

[Editor's note: This information is related in great detail because there was a photograph of Ernest Holmes and Dr. Frank Robinson speaking before a mass audience at the Philharmonic Auditorium in Los Angeles, an event which took place September 21 through 25, 1941. The affirmation on the headline of this "American Spiritual Awakening" publication read, "Let there be immediate peace on earth through the power of the spirit of the living God." After this took place, the decision to withdraw from the movement was made by the Board as described above.]

· 1945 ·

On April 5, 1945, a special meeting was called. Trustees Smith, McBean, Benshimol, Griffin, and Haughey were present. Absent were Trustees Armor, Holmes, and Newell. The purpose of the meeting was to introduce Dr. Stanley Bartlett to the Board of Trustees. He was being hired to handle the Building Fund Campaign and reorganization of the membership, and was given full reign to do whatever he felt necessary to handle these matters. He would take office beginning April 16, 1945, and would be present at Institute headquarters Monday, Tuesday, and Wednesday of each week.[9]

On May 16, the Board discussed a Regional School of the Institute of Religious Science in Cincinnati, Ohio, under the leadership of Dr. J. Arthur Twyne. It was in the experimental stage, with permanent policies not yet fixed or worked out. Holmes moved that "the group under the leadership of Dr. Twyne should not be designated as 'colored' in the Science of Mind Magazine or in any other literature that we may have. This is also to apply to any other group of this nature."[10] The motion was carried.

A special meeting was called on May 22, 1945 to entertain a request by Dr. J. Lowrey Fendrich, Jr. for a chapter charter for his study group in Washington, D.C. The president, based on the recommendation of the Committee on Field Activities, moved that the charter be granted.[11] At the June 20 meeting, recognition was granted to ten additional practitioners.[12] At the September 19 regular meeting, the chairman "submitted a recommendation from the Committee on Education that the following list of practitioners be approved as teachers of Religious Science": Jennie Davis Brown, Ivy Crane Shelhamer, Daisy Mae Beckett, Erma C. Wendt, Marjorie Fletcher, Raymond Charles Barker, Ernest Holmes, Clarence Mayer, Thomas B. Baird, Richleigh P. Crowley, Z. Fay McCall, Elizabeth Larson, Harold Fowler Gerrard, Reginald C. Armor, J. Arthur Twyne, Anita Schofield, Frederick W. Bailes, Alta Turk Everett, John Hefferlin, Hester Brunt, Carmelita Trowbridge, Isobel Poulin, Robert Bitzer, J. Lowrey Fendrich, Jr., Joseph Larson, Lora B. Holman, Stanley W. Bartlett, Elizabeth Carrick-Cook, William B. Tubbs, Dan Custer, Edgar White Burrill, Idella M. Chadwick, Maude Allison Lathem. The approval of the teachers named was granted.[13]

At the October 17 meeting concerning the Cincinnati Regional School, the following was reported:

Trustee Armor explained that Dr. Fendrich had taken it for granted that Cincinnati was to be considered as a Regional School of the Institute, even though at that time it was not a chapter. However, certain difficulties [had] developed regarding [this]. The President submitted the following resolution with reference to teaching at Cincinnati, taken from the minutes of the special meeting of the Committee on Education of September 11, 1945.

"It was moved, seconded[,] and passed that Cincinnati be set up as a Regional School for a specific period of time to conduct instruction for credit by the Institute. On a temporary basis they will conduct class work and the clinic leading to a practitioner certificate, the results to be passed on by the Institute and the certificates to be issued by the Institute. This right to conduct the educational program will expire at a certain time, this time to be decided on by the Committee on Education."¹⁴

At this same meeting, Armor "brought up the question of establishing dummy corporations in every state of the country in order to protect the name of The Institute of Religious Science. The President stated that [attorney Arion] Lewis was now working on this, getting the requirements from every state as to just what must be done under the circumstances."¹⁵

At the November 21 meeting, Dan Custer was recognized for conducting a very successful Sunday morning meeting at the Institute building. The organization was doing well financially, it was reported, and everything was growing. September had been the slowest month of the year, but it appeared everything would be fine by the beginning of the next year, 1946. The president's report also noted that Dr. Raymond Barker had opened his lectures in New York City with an attendance of over two hundred on his opening night, and that the work there looked very encouraging. It was also reported that Dr. Stanley Bartlett was returning from Denver, Colorado, where he had interviewed Dr. Harvey Hardman and Dr. Wanbig about their coming into the organization. Dr. Bartlett stated that the development of the group was coming along nicely and that he would submit a full report on his return. Dr. Fredrick Bailes had been writing thumbnail sketches or outlines of Sunday talks given by Dr. Bailes at the monthly meetings of Southern California ministers. They were "so fine," it was thought, that they decided to make mimeograph copies sent to every chapter leader each month.¹⁶

It was recommended on December 19 that Joseph Murphy be ordained a minister of Religious Science. Murphy was to act as the leader of the Rochester, New York chapter. Additional practitioner's certificates were granted to Geraldine Usher, Madge Bartlett, Florence Lee Holtzman, William Barth, Marie Leone Green, and George W. Allison.¹⁷

[Editor's note: Over the years, in the course of visiting many churches, I would be shown, with great pride, certificates hanging on the walls of churches designating them variously "Chapters," "Teaching Chapters," and "Churches" in affiliation with the Institute of Religious Science and Philosophy. Further in this history, we shall discover what occasioned these and other designations.]

· 1946 ·

The first meeting of 1946 was held on February 20, with fifteen new practitioners being recognized. There was also one teacher recognition, Lucille Graham, as well as recognition of new study groups.[18]

The president reported that Holmes had suggested changes in the administrative setup of the Institute. He wanted to dispense with the different committees as they then stood, namely the Committee on Education and the Committee on Field Activities, and create an overall committee to be known as the Executive Committee, with the following members: Reginald Armor, director of the Extension Education work; Dr. Fendrich, director of Education; Dr. Bailes, director of Field Activities; Dan Custer, director of Radio Activities; Dr. Bartlett, director of Finance and Membership. Each of these persons was to be a member of the Executive Committee, each representing his respective department. The motion carried.[19]

NAME CHANGE TO "CHURCH OF RELIGIOUS SCIENCE" IS APPROVED

At the May 13, 1946 business meeting of the Religious Science Chapter Association, Holmes suggested that since the majority of the leaders agreed that the devotional service be called "Church of Religious Science," each leader should recommend to his or her congregation that the name "Church of Religious Science" be adopted, explaining that the name "Institute of Religious Science" would be retained for the educational activities, also informing their membership that the Institute had purchased the corporation known as the "Church of Religious Science" and that they had full authority to the use of the name. This motion was carried.[20]

The name of each chapter would be the "Church of Religious Science" followed by the chapter name, such as "– Hollywood." Holmes suggested that somewhere on the promotional folder created by each chapter they should state that they are a chapter of the Institute of Religious Science of Los Angeles, and that the classes be advertised as "Classes in the Science of Mind." This motion was carried.[21]

The chairman asked that the matter of uniform subjects for Sunday mornings be discussed—whether the present policy should be continued or whether each leader should choose his or her own subject so long as they dealt with Science of Mind. After a general discussion, Holmes suggested that the chair would appoint a committee to make up fifty-two general subjects covering "the textbook." This motion was carried. John Hefferlin moved that the customary practice of uniform subjects be absolutely adhered to. This motion was not voted on. Hefferlin also asked that in case a leader could not attend a Chapter Association meeting, it be made a priority to appoint a delegate in his place. No action was taken.[22]

Two days later—May 15, 1946—there was a meeting of the Executive Committee, at which the resolution of February 20 concerning an Executive Committee as proposed by Ernest Holmes was placed into formal motion by attorney Arion Lewis, and was adopted.[23]

At this meeting, Haughey also reported that the organization now had the right to use the name "Church of Religious Science." He said that the majority of the chapters wished to use this name and had passed a resolution to that effect in March 1944. At the last meeting of the Chapter Association, it had been decided that the devotional services would be called "Church of Religious Science" and the educational functions be called "Institute of Religious Science." Up until this time, it was reported,

> [T]he organization had not been able to use the name "Church of Religious Science" in Los Angeles because it belonged to another corporation. The Chairman reported that the Institute had negotiated with the officers of this former Church of Religious Science and had purchased their corporation.
>
> The chairman reported that [attorney Arion] Lewis was now formulating the transfer of the constitution, by-laws, etc., and that same would be presented to the Board of Trustees at a later meeting. Mr. Haughey also informed the Board that any chapter wishing to use the name "Church of Religious Science" must apply to the Board of Trustees of the Institute of Religious Science at Los Angeles.[24]

The Practitioners League of the Institute of Religious Science wanted to create its own constitution and bylaws. This request was tabled.[25]

At the June 11, 1946 meeting, "the chairman read the report from the Sunday School Department for the month of May. The average weekly attendance was 57, average collection $8.92, average per capita 15¢."[26] Dr. Frederick Bailes made a request to begin an Institute chapter in downtown Los Angeles. He presented his case and stated that if a chapter charter was not granted he would request that his resignation be accepted. He was excused from the meeting for further discussion by the Board. After thorough discussion, it was decided that the Board "could not grant such a charter to Dr. Bailes or to anyone else at this time."[27] [Editor's note: The chapter would have been only a few miles from the Institute. Dr. Bailes resigned. He had a very large following that met at the Ebell Theater for many years.]

At this point, chapters were notified to request a name change to "Church of Religious Science" for their specific chapters. For a long time, the Santa Barbara chapter was the only one to make the request.[28] After that, requests came in from chapters in Santa Anita, Hollywood, Burbank, and Glendale.

Concerning postgraduate studies, it was decided that

> The Department of Education shall provide advanced courses of study in Science of Mind, Metaphysics, Psychology[,] and allied subjects to be given at the Institute. All curricula therefor shall be subject to the approval of the Board of Trustees.
>
> The courses of study provided for . . . shall be known as the Post Graduate Courses and the following grades for satisfactory completion of work therein shall be granted by the Institute:
>
> A. Bachelor of Religious Science
>
> B. Master of Religious Science
>
> C. Doctor of Religious Science
>
> The Department of Education, subject to the approval of the Board of Trustees, shall prescribe the courses of study, entrance requirements, and all administrative matters relating thereto, that shall be required for each grade of recognition . . .
>
> The recognition . . . shall be granted, upon recommendation of the Department of Education, to regularly enrolled students who have satisfactorily completed the course or courses of study prescribed for such recognition. Such recognition shall be evidenced in appropriate written form under the authority and direction of the Board of Trustees, which shall be delivered to the person so recognized.[29]

There had been discussions with attorney Arion Lewis about giving degrees. He informed the board that they could not legally use the word "degree" but could instead say, for example, "The Board of Trustees, by virtue of authority vested in it, has recognized [name of conferee] as a Bachelor [or Master, or Doctor] of Religious Science."[30]

· 1947 ·

A BRIEF HISTORY OF THE RELIGIOUS SCIENCE ORGANIZATION

William Haughey became a trustee in 1939 and chairman of the Board in 1940. The following is his recollection of the beginnings of the organization:

At first, the Sunday services were held at the Ambassador Theater and the weekday meetings were in a building located at the corner of Wilshire Boulevard and Carondelet. The services at the Ambassador held 400 people. They moved to the Ebell Theater that held about 1,300 people. The lectures became very popular, and the Ebell was overflowing. They then moved to the Biltmore Ballroom, which held about 2,200 people. They remained there a short time because the Biltmore Hotel changed the ballroom into the Bowl, and they had no place for us. They then moved to the Wiltern Theater at the corner of Wilshire Boulevard and Western Avenue, which held 2,240 people, and remained there for ten years, filling the theater to capacity every Sunday morning. The reason they had to leave there was because the Wiltern Theater decided they wanted to have a "first-run house" and therefore they wanted to open earlier and that did not leave time for a morning service.

[Editor's note: During the church service, the theater would prepare for the Sunday matinee and begin popping popcorn. I remember the fragrance being very appealing to the congregation.]

There was no other place in Los Angeles large enough to hold the congregation. So they had to split the congregation; they rented the Ebell Theater and the Time Theater from the Friday Morning Club to accommodate those who could not go to the Ebell. These were the two largest theaters in Los Angeles. The classes, healing groups, and meditation were all held at the Institute on West 6th Street. The Science of Mind magazine now has subscribers all over the world, with subscriptions going to New Zealand, Australia, South Africa, England, and so forth.

AN ASSOCIATE DEAN IS APPOINTED

At the August 13, 1947 meeting, new business included the appointment of an associate dean. A resolution was approved creating the position of Associate Dean as an administrative officer for Ernest Holmes, dean and for the president. Ernest Holmes then appointed Dr. J. Lowrey Fendrich, Jr. as Associate Dean and Dr. Stanley Bartlett as director of the Education Department. This was ratified by the Board.[31] [Editor's note: Over the years, there were times when the charter of a chapter was withdrawn. One of these was the Santa Monica chapter, another was San Diego, First Chapter. They were instructed never to use the "Institute of Religious Science and Philosophy" in their name and to return the charter each held. Circumstances surrounding these withdrawals were not published.]

At the meeting of September 17, 1947, it was decided that,

> As one of the activities for the Bay District of Northern California, a school and college, exactly duplicating the work of the school and College at Los Angeles to be established either at San Francisco or Oakland, to be determined by Dr. Dan Custer upon his becoming Regional Director.
>
> Therefore be it resolved: That Dr. Dan Custer be appointed Dean of the Regional College in the Bay District of Northern California.[32]

At the September 17 meeting, it was also reported that Holmes would begin speaking at the Beverly Hills Theater in November, replacing Dr. Custer, who would be going to Northern California. Dr. Custer said that he would be speaking at the Oakland chapter, as its leader, Mrs. Beckett, was planning to resign.[33] [Editor's note: For further information, see meeting minutes March 23, 1950.]

In the November 19 meeting, new business concerned the annual conference for chapter leaders, Southern California Chapter Association serving as hosts. Haughey reported, "the conference will begin Monday morning January 26th [1948] in the Fiesta Room [downstairs social hall at the Institute] and run through January 30th, with lunch served each day. There will be morning and afternoon sessions and the program is now being drafted. The Ebell Theatre has been engaged for January 26, 1948 and there would be no banquet. Leaders are being asked to participate in the program."[34]

To become a practitioner of Religious Science, clinical training was required. This course was conducted by Reginald C. Armor, Clarence Mayer, and Idella Chadwick. The Clinic consisted of thirty-six hours in practical class instruction plus questions and answers arising in the practice of Science of Mind. The Clinic fee was $25.[35]

· 1948 ·

The sixth annual meeting of the Religious Science Chapter Association (Southern California) was held on Monday, January 26 and Tuesday, January 27, 1948. During these days of meetings, there were a variety of "conferences" for people to attend. Tuesday's list included "Right Thinking in Business":

> This conference is primarily for men; however, just as it implies, all business people can come. If you have a Men's Club, send delegates from your Men's Club to this conference. Send as many as you desire. The Leader of this conference will be Lawrence Atwood of Pasadena, prominent businessman and member of the Pasadena Chapter.[36]

Other conferences on the program included "Methods of Teaching Literature for Your Sunday School Teachers"; "Young People's Activities"; and "What the Women's Club Can Do in the Chapter."[37]

"We want each delegate from the Women's Club to attend this conference," the program said. "Additional subjects will be parliamentary law, a model club in action, its educational and cultural opportunities, and financial opportunities. Send as many women as possible. Leader is Mabel Kinney. The Silent Healing Department: send representatives of your silent workers."[38]

In October 1947, there was an "Expansion Fund" developed so that people from all parts of the world could send contributions toward the expansion of the Religious Science Chapter Association. Haughey reported, "On the wall behind the desk of Charles Kinnear hangs a map on which he indicated where donations were coming from. He states that 'these gifts have come from 33 of the 48 states. There are no chapters included in these donations. In fact, 40% of the locations on the map represent a Fellow of International Religious Science living where there is no chapter. This means that the donor keeps in touch with the Institute through the *Science of Mind* magazine, Home Study Course, the Department of Healing or one of the other departments.'"

This created a special challenge. At the annual conference of January 1948, it was decided that the first step in an expansion program would be the writing of a constitution for the conducting of church and field work through an association of Religious Science churches. A committee was appointed to prepare a constitution. The constitution committee was to make a report at the conference to convene in January 1949. The committee was authorized to use the money from the Expansion Fund for this work. The work by both the expansion committee and the constitution committee was recognized and thanks was given to the committee's members: "With the formation of the International Association of Religious Science Churches and the adoption of a constitution, unlimited opportunity for the advancement of Religious Science will be made possible and we know that you will continue to have a part in it."

· 1949 ·

A resolution passed at a meeting held March 24, 1949 required that chapter status be abolished and that all chapters be notified and advised that the abolition of chapter status was for the purpose of enabling each existing chapter to become a completely independent and autonomous church organization and to enable it to become a member of the International Association of Religious Science Churches.[39]

Over the years, many gifts of property and stocks have been donated to the Institute. Stocks were contributed toward a special Radio Fund for Dr. Holmes. Also, John F. Alcott, a personal friend of Holmes, left $5,000 to the Institute in his will.

In 1949, land in Michigan was left to the Institute. "Trustee Bartlett reported an application for an oil leak on 40 acres of land conveyed to the Institute by Mrs. Ida B. Bradshaw. The Board agreed to decline the lease for the time being, pending word of confident sources in Michigan before taking any action."[40]

THE HOME STUDY COURSE IS ACCREDITED

The Home Study Course was created by Holmes and Armor and was very popular as a series of lessons that could be mailed to a student when there was no church nearby. Students would receive a lesson, read the textbook, answer the questions, and return their answers to the Institute. They would then receive the next lesson.

On September 10, 1949, Armor wrote to Dr. Robert Bitzer of the Hollywood Chapter of the Church of Religious Science. He said, in part,

> There are...many Church Leaders who wish to use it in connection with the Textbook lectures. Also, many individual students desire to have this helpful material as a reference library and an aid in their studies. A plan has been arranged whereby a student who

is taking, or has taken[,] the First Year College may receive the Home Study lessons only, on a cultural, non-credit basis. These enrollments are handled only through the Churches, at a special tuition fee of $50.00. All payments are sent in by the Church and the manuscripts are sent directly to the Church for distribution to the students.

If the full tuition is paid at the time of enrollment, all manuscripts will be shipped in one mailing. If more desirable, the student may make four payments of $12.50 each at thirty day intervals; thirteen manuscripts being mailed for each payment. This special "cultural" price of $50.00 is made possible by the fact that there is no service required on the part of the Institute here in Los Angeles, other than shipping material to the Church; no certificate of credit is involved and postage for weekly mailings is eliminated. . . .

[T]he Home Study credit [is] equal to three-fifths of the First Year College work. You will have some students who will want to avail themselves of the opportunity to take part of their work by Home Study. This arrangement is particularly advantageous where students have taken two or three terms and have to move to some place where resident class work is not available. Also, there may be cases where students could not adjust their time to resident class work.[41]

[Editor's note: The previous is excerpted from a letter to Dr. Robert Bitzer, but I believe that this, or a similar letter, went out to all Churches.]

Next is a letter from the Institute of Religious Science addressed to all graduates of the Institute of Religious Science, signed by Stanley Bartlett, Dean, College of Religious Science:

We are happy to enclose the first year college calendar in our 1949–1950 class work. In "Religion," this year provides five units of study; each tuition is at a cost of $15.00. Each unit involves 24 hours of instruction. There will be day and night classes, each being conducted twice a week. For the first time there will be special emphasis placed on metaphysical Bible studies. Both units one and two feature the textbook, Science of Mind, and Bible studies. For some time we have been eager to give our students more Bible training and we anticipate the revised curriculum will be greatly appreciated by all students of Religious Science.

The *Personal Improvement Course,* a series of twenty-four lessons, was referenced in a bulletin on August 14, 1946. There were to be two lessons per week for twelve weeks. It was not to be publicized at that time. Another course which had been very successful was *Your Undiscovered Power:* "This ten-lesson course has been most successful as a beginner's course. The tuition is $2.00. Owing to the extremely low price, no commission will be paid on this course."

THE IARSC IS ESTABLISHED

After the January 1949 conference, where the constitution for the International Association of Religious Science Churches (IARSC) was approved, there was a letter dated January 26, 1949 from Charles Kinnear to each of the chapter leaders who was affiliated with the IARSC:

> The report of the annual conference will be ready for you in about ten days' time.
>
> Rev. Lora Holman has called our attention to the fact that all organizations paying $600 or more in salary or rent, must make an information report both to the Internal Revenue Department and, for California chapters, to the Franchise Tax Commissioner.
>
> These reports must be in by February 15. Secure your forms for the Internal Revenue information from your nearest Internal Revenue office. You will need form 1096 Annual Information Return 1948. Also form 1099 Individual Information Return (to whom paid) is to be sent to the Processing Division, Kansas City, Missouri. The address is given on the forms. It would be wise to order two copies of 1096 and two copies for each of the individual returns you must make on 1099.
>
> In California secure your California report from the Franchise Tax Commissioner. Regarding Form 596 for the Annual Information Return and Form 599 (to whom paid) order the same quantity as for the Internal Revenue Report.
>
> The California report is to be sent to the Franchise Tax Commissioner, Sacramento 14, California not later than February 15.
>
> Sincerely,
>
> Charles Kinnear[42]

[Editor's note: I'm sure Rev. Lora Holman's guidance was very helpful.]

On June 23, 1949, a resolution was signed by Holmes, Haughey, and Estelle Ruckman:

[T]he Institute of Religious Science is a California corporation and affiliates itself with the International Association of Religious Science Churches, a California corporation . . . [B]e it further resolved that the minister, the chairman and the secretary of the Board of Trustees are hereby authorized and empowered to execute for and on behalf of this corporation [the Institute] any and all documents necessary to effectuate such affiliation.

[Editor's note: This, then, is the formal affiliation of the Institute of Religious Science with the IARSC—the same kind of affiliation as with the churches.]

Under the above arrangement, the Institute remains in charge of all class work, who can teach the classes, and what is being taught.

Application for [the status of] Practitioner of Religious Science may be made by a candidate who qualifies under one of the following categories:

1. Who has successfully completed the First Year College work (Bachelor of Religious Science), which includes Clinical Training at the Los Angeles Institute or at a church authorized as a Teaching Chapter of the Institute.

2. Who has successfully completed the fifty two week Home Study Course in the Science of Mind plus that unit of the First Year College embodying Clinical Training.

3. Who holds a Practitioner certificate or equivalent in some organization recognized by the Institute, such as Christian Science, Unity, Divine Science, etc. and has successfully completed the fifty two week Home Study Course in the Science of Mind.

At the June 23 meeting of the IARSC, Articles of Incorporation and Bylaws were approved and then sent to the Members of the Representative Council of the IARSC.

The Institute of Religious Science requested a church charter from the IARSC, thus establishing affiliation with the IARSC, stating:

You are hereby authorized and empowered to execute for and on behalf of this corporation any and all documents necessary to effectuate such affiliation. We therefore request the church charter from the IARSC for our church organization.

BOOKS PUBLISHED DURING THE 1940S

Books and booklets published by Ernest Holmes in the 1940s: *Your Invisible Power* (1940); *Mind Remakes Your World* (1941; edited by Ernest Holmes and includes an essay by him); *New Thought Terms and Their Meanings* (1942); *This Thing Called Life* (1943); *Lessons in Spiritual Mind Healing* (1943); *Pray and Prosper* (1944); *What Religious Science Teaches* (1944); *Give Us This Day* (1947); *This Thing Called You* (1948); and *Words That Heal Today* (1949).

A TYPICAL CLASS BROCHURE

MAJOR DAY COURSE BULLETIN 1945–1946, Institute of Religious Science

25th Annual Major Course in the Science of Mind and Allied Subjects

October 1, 1945 to June 14, 1946, 3251 W. 6th St., Los Angeles, California.

These are a series of special lectures: What Is Science of Mind; Spiritual Mind Healing and Mental Suggestion; Technique for Mental Treatment; Affirmations and Denials in Mental Treatment; Science, Prayer and Faith; The Principle of Divine Guidance; Spiritual Prototypes as Conceived by Plato, Jesus and Emerson; Science of Mind and the New Psychology, the Relationship between Science of Mind and the New Psychology; The Ego, the Id and the Super Ego; The Divine Urge Operating through Man; Theory of Repression, Why We Are Buried Alive; Fears and Phobias, Faith Can Overcome Fears; Psychic Fixations; Loose Him and Let Him Go; Catharsis and Chemicalization, Curative Action of Spiritual Thought; Psychological Escapes Met Only through Spiritual Realization; Conscience and Conflict, Why There Is Belief in the Devil and Hell and a God of Vengeance; Spiritual Significance of the Transference, Being Back to God;

Spiritual Purpose of Analysis; Coming to Self-Awareness – Know the Truth and the Truth Shall Set You Free; Evolution of the Libido, Conscious Union of Man with God; The Psychic Cause of Success and Failure; Specializing the Law of Cause and Effect; Law of Mental Identity; Divine Presence and Divine Principle; This Psychic Life of Ours; Spiritual Realization and Psychic Hallucination; Adam and Christ – The Serpent and the Savior; Teachers of the Illumined; Metaphysical Charts – Three Lectures.

In addition to the above, Dr. Holmes will give a talk on Phineas P. Quimby and New Thought. Also four special lectures on Emerson: Essays on History, Self-Reliance, Compensation and Spiritual Laws.

There are also supplemental lectures by Frederick Bailes, Dan Custer, Ivy C. Shelhamer, Leslie Violet, Rabbi Ernest Trattner, Fitz Kunkel, Hans Nordewin von Koerber, Ph.D., Herbert Popenoe, and W. Ballentine Henley, President of the College of Osteopathic Physicians and Surgeons, Professor of Medical Jurisprudence, and Educational Organizer.

[Editor's note: Henley later became the President of the Church of Religious Science.]

These lectures are given in addition to the regular class work which takes place on Monday, Wednesday, and Friday for two hours each shared with two speakers, one hour each, i.e.: Hour one on Monday October 1st at 10:00 a.m. is Ernest Holmes speaking on What Is Science of Mind and hour two on Monday at 11:00 a.m. is Frederick Bailes (textbook), Universal Love and Law; Wednesday, October 3rd, 10:00 a.m. is Reginald Armor, Road to Freedom (textbook), Ivy Shelhamer next hour, and so forth. This first term begins October 1st and ends December 14th. Second term begins January 4th and ends March 22nd, and the third term begins April 2nd and ends June 14th.

5

The 1950s:
Difficult Years for the IARSC

PART I: 1951–1953

Hitherto we have inverted the true order of cause and effect; now, by carefully considering the real nature of the Principle of Causation in itself … we return to the true order and adopt a new method of thinking in accordance with it.

Thomas Troward, *Doré Lectures*[1]

THE MEN'S CLUB

An announcement in the Men's Club publication, "Green Sheet Monthly," of the Institute of Religious Science, states that the president is Bob Lockard and the editor is Clint Bacon. The purpose is given as: "The Men's Club is an organization of free men dedicated to the principles that each individual is architect of his own destiny and that health, happiness, and prosperity are beyond the reach of no one."

In the minutes of the February 13, 1950 International Association of Religious Science Churches, (IARSC) Representatives Council meeting, there is a report on the name "Church of Religious Science":

> At this time a motion was made and carried giving instruction that charters from all the different churches should be returned to the Church of Religious Science. The name on the certificate is

to be corrected to read: _____ Church of Religious Science, City and State. The blank is for the numerical accommodation of 1st, 2nd, 3rd, as the case may be when there is more than one church in one city, i.e., "First Church of Religious Science, Los Angeles, California."[2]

A SAN FRANCISCO BAY AREA REGIONAL SCHOOL

Dan Custer, of the Regional School in San Francisco, wanted to have a Sunday evening service in Berkeley, across the bay. However, the IARSC wished to eliminate the position Regional Director in San Francisco and discontinue their regional school there.[3] The Institute Board of Trustees would give direction concerning college courses; a memorandum from the secretary of the Board directed that the Director of Education be instructed to prepare a resolution eliminating the regional school and the office of Regional Director in San Francisco.[4]

Whereas at the regular meeting of September 17, 1947 of the Board of Trustees of the Institute of Religious Science, it was resolved that as one of the activities of the Bay District of Northern California, a school and college exactly duplicating the work of the school and the work of the Institute at Los Angeles be established in the Bay District, either at San Francisco or Oakland as determined by Dr. Dan Custer upon becoming its Regional Director;

Therefore, be it resolved, that Dr. Dan Custer be appointed Dean of the Regional College of the Bay District of Northern California."

Whereas, the currently authorized and functioning Association of Religious Science Churches is responsible for church activities in the field;

Therefore be it resolved that the co-director classification be abolished as of June 30, 1950;

And be it further resolved that the first year college work be conducted at all teaching points in accord with the established policy for such teaching; and that second year college work be authorized only when and where the Board of Trustees of the Institute of Religious Science at Los Angeles determines it to be needed and qualifications for teaching fully met.

Motion was carried.[5]

At the April 27, 1950 meeting, the subject of regional schools again arose.

> A motion was made by Trustee Lewis that the Board defer the subject of the possible continuation of Regional Schools, particularly in San Francisco, to the Executive Committee for further consideration and report if possible at the next meeting of the board. Motion was seconded and carried.[6]

Along with a recommendation for Elmer Gifford to receive a doctorate recognition was a recognition of Ralph Waldo Trine of Claremont College.[7]

At an IARSC meeting on May 5, the subject of ordaining ministers was discussed. It was moved:

> That we empower a committee, Jack Fostinis, Lora Holman, and Anita Schofield, Jack Fostinis acting as presiding officer, to meet with the Executive Committee of the Institute and inform them that as a church organization we shall exercise our power to ordain ministers of Religious Science upon advice of the Education Department of the Institute that the applicant has met the educational requirements, and that the certificate will be issued by the Representative Council in the name of the IARSC. The motion was carried.[8]

By this time, Fenwicke Holmes was in California and had started a church in Oakland. [Editor's note: This occurred in the summer of 1950, possibly around September.]

QUALIFICATIONS TO TEACH ACCREDITED CLASSES ARE ANNOUNCED

A letter to the Board of Trustees of all chartered Science of Mind Churches signed by Fletcher Harding, Director of Education, under the letterhead of the Institute of Religious Science and Philosophy, dated October 5, 1950, reads:

> Dear Friends:
> The Department of Education of the Institute of Religious Science, Los Angeles, is enclosing a formal application for the use of your Church. The approval of this application, by the Board of

Trustees, Institute of Religious Science, Los Angeles, will qualify your Church officially as an Accredited Teaching Chapter of the College of Religious Science, Los Angeles.

As you are no doubt informed, the College of Religious Science, Los Angeles, still holds the Teaching Franchise for Accredited Religious Science class work. The First Year College work has been presented in our various Churches in the past. It is intended that this policy shall continue. However, in order to more closely integrate the teaching program that it may become increasingly effective, we are requesting each Religious Science Church to file the enclosed application blank-agreement. This will clearly establish a license for your Church to teach Accredited College classes under the rules, regulations, etc., of the Board of Trustees at the Institute of Religious Science in Los Angeles, and its Educational Department. Further, it will give us a clearer picture of our faculty members as they are located throughout the Nation.

We feel this is a step that will strengthen the teaching program and ultimately benefit the Churches who enter into this agreement with us.[9]

RADIO PROGRAMS

At the June 22, 1950 meeting, regarding the Radio Program:

Trustee Holmes reported a meeting of the Radio Committee on the subject of the Radio Program, at which plans were made and discussed for keeping the program on the air, proposing that it be incorporated as a separate non-profit organization to carry it more effectively across the country, and that a representative be financed to contact people who wish to contribute to a worthy tax-exempt fund. The Board approved Dr. Holmes's recommendation and resolved that the Radio Committee should proceed to handle the enterprise as a separate entity.[10]

At the July 20, 1950 meeting of the Radio Committee,

Trustee Atwood reported that the Radio Committee felt that the Sunday radio program should continue as an Institute program for the time being. Motion made and carried that the

Radio Committee be authorized to proceed with the business management of all Institute radio programs with full authority to act as far as the radio program is concerned, and that the Executive Committee be advised of their proposal and decisions from time to time to consummate same.[11]

RECOGNITION AT UNITED NATIONS

At the September 21, 1950 Board meeting, Dr. Fletcher Harding reported that Dr. Raymond Barker had introduced the Institute's literature at the UN Assembly Headquarters in New York. A motion was made by Atwood that a letter of commendation be sent to Dr. Barker in New York for doing so. This was seconded by Armor and carried.[12]

IARSC IS APPROVED TO ORDAIN MINISTERS

On October 19, 1950, there was a resolution regarding the ordination of ministers by Religious Science churches.

> Trustee Armor, acting for the Credential Department, presented the following resolution, in agreement with the International Association of Religious Science Churches, and moved that it be approved and adopted by this board:
> "Whereas it is the desire of the Institute to stimulate full cooperation between the Institute and the International Association of Religious Science Churches in their common purpose of carrying the ministry and our philosophy to an ever increasing field, therefore, be it resolved that the International Association of Religious Science Churches perform the duty and function of ordaining persons to be ministers of Religious Science to serve in churches which are members of the IARSC."[13]

This motion was seconded and carried.

At this same meeting, Dr. J. Lowrey Fendrich, whose Sunday morning services at the Uptown Theater in Los Angeles constituted a department of the Institute, requested that this relationship be severed so that his group could become an affiliated church of the IARSC.[14] [Editor's note: At this time, services being held at the Uptown Theater, Belmont Theater, Wiltern Theater, and Beverly Hills Theater were not independent works but rather *departments* of the Institute. Thus, all income went to the Institute, and all salaries and other expenses were paid by the Institute.]

HORNADAY ASSUMES RESPONSIBILITY FOR THE DAILY RADIO PROGRAM

At the December 21, 1950 meeting, there were two important subjects discussed. Under new business,

> Trustee Atwood reported that after careful study and consideration of the daily radio program of the Institute and with the approval of Ernest Holmes, effective January 2, 1951, Dr. William Hornaday is employed to carry on the daily radio program for five days a week, and recommended that this appointment be approved by the board. Dr. Atwood stated, "There is no discontent with the program as it is, but it was felt that it would be advisable for the benefit of the entire Institute and that it is a full-time job."
>
> A motion was made and carried that the committee's temporary employment of Dr. Hornaday be approved by the board.[15]

The second subject of interest at the December meeting was that of electing a new president of the Institute.

> Trustee Holmes tendered his oral resignation as president of the Institute. Motion was made and carried to accept with regret the resignation of Dr. Holmes. The Vice Chairman then nominated Trustee [Norman] Van Valkenburgh as President. Trustee Lewis moved that the nominations be closed and that Trustee Van Valkenburgh be unanimously elected as President of the Institute. The motion was seconded and carried.[16]

William Hornaday had had private training in Religious Science with Dr. Holmes. Armor presented the application of Hornaday to become a licensed Practitioner of Religious Science, and recommended that it be approved subject to the completion of his credentials. The application was referred back to the Credential Department for clarification and presentation at a future time.[17]

· 1951 ·

Dr. Fletcher Harding gave a presentation on Dianetics (Scientology) at the 1951 Congress.

HOLMES FORGIVES $6,000 LOAN TO INSTITUTE

At the February 15, 1951 meeting, Armor reported that the following agreement had been arranged with Holmes:

> This is to certify that I [Holmes] have this date cancelled notes due payable to me from the Institute of Religious Science and Philosophy Incorporated in the amount of $6,000 . . . leaving notes payable to me as of this date in the amount of $2,500 . . .
>
> Signed, Ernest Holmes[18]

A motion was made and carried that the board accept Dr. Holmes's generous offer with gratitude and appreciation.

PROPERTY PURCHASES

At this time, the Institute was interested in purchasing the property adjoining the Institute building on the west side. The property was for sale, and the committee believed it advisable at this time to acquire it. It was suggested that representatives of Aetna Insurance Company, now holding a loan to the Institute, be contacted to appraise the property with the idea of increasing the amount of the loan, in the event they wanted to purchase the additional property. Atwood was authorized to investigate.[19]

At the March 15, 1951 meeting, concerning the purchase of the adjoining property, Atwood reported having contacted Coldwell Banker Company regarding a loan and having been advised that their insurance company would not be interested. Atwood also stated that he had talked with the owner of the property concerning the possibility of the owner's financing part of the loan and that he would report back about the owner's decision. Atwood said that he would appreciate hearing from any of the Board members who might know of anyone interested in a three-year loan to the Institute of approximately $20,000. No decision was made.[20]

At the April 19, 1951 meeting, Holmes once again came forward as a generous financial donor:

> Trustee Atwood reported that the amount of $1,400 is due the IARSC for church dues and that Ernest Holmes has offered to pay the amount of $700 toward the amount from a bequest to the Institute by Sydney Alcott.[21]

HORNADAY BECOMES A MEMBER OF THE INSTITUTE'S MINISTERIAL STAFF

At the May 3, 1951 Board meeting,

> Trustee Armor, Credentials Department, recommended that William H. D. Hornaday be officially authorized as a member of the Institute ministerial staff and requested that the IARSC grant him recognition as Minister in the Gospel of Religious Science, based upon the recognition of his previous ordination as Minister of the Gospel of Calvary College in 1939. Motion duly made and carried to approve the recommendation.
>
> Trustee Armor also recommended that Dr. William H. D. Hornaday be appointed a member of the teaching faculty of the Institute, having completed the academic requirements, and that the appointment be made effective as soon as he receives his teaching certificate.[22]

ANOTHER LOAN IS OFFERED BY HOLMES

Also at the May 3, 1951 meeting, a resolution was made by Arion Lewis:

> Whereas this corporation desires to make a loan of $10,000 payable in three years at 5%, and to execute its promissory note and trustees, securing the payment thereof on the following described property, and
>
> Whereas Ernest S. Holmes and Hazel B. Holmes have offered to make said loan to the corporation;
>
> Now, therefore, be it resolved that said loan be made and that the president and secretary of this corporation be hereby authorized and directed to execute and deliver the corporation promissory note, payable to Ernest S. Holmes and Hazel B. Holmes, as joint tenants, in the sum of $10,000 ... payable with interest at the rate of 5% per annum ... three years after date. Interest payable on the unpaid balance semi-annually, with reservation of the right to pay all or any part of said principal and accumulated interest at any time after one year; and that the corporation trust deed securing payment of said note be made, executed, and delivered conveying the following described real estate. ...

[Editor's note: This took place after Coldwell Banker denied a loan to the Institute to purchase property, presumably the property discussed at the March 15 meeting, above.]

RELIGIOUS SCIENCE GOES TO ISRAEL AND EUROPE

In the October 14, 1951 meeting of the IARSC Representative Council, it was noted that a Mrs. Nadia Williams was expecting to sail to the State of Israel, to start a work "at her own expense in establishing a Religious Science Center. The Council commended her for her decision and gave her permission to establish in Israel whatever type of Religious Science activity she deemed wise and best in her judgment."[23]

Spruit reported that a Mr. and Mrs. Inglis were contemplating a trip to Europe "for the purpose of propagating the message of Religious Science, and that they were planning to remain there as long as two years, if need be, all at their own expense. The Council voted to commend Mr. and Mrs. Inglis for their plan, and extended to them the privilege of representing [the IARSC's] cause."[24]

In an announcement at the July 26 meeting, it was reported that Sunday services had begun at the Uptown Theater. Johansen, chairman of the Church Committee, suggested that Board members be in attendance at the inaugural appearance of William Hornaday at the theater.[25] At the August 5 meeting, Shipley suggested that Johansen, in his capacity as chairman of the Church Committee, notify all Board members, inviting them to attend and ascertaining whether they could attend.[26]

SECOND-YEAR COLLEGE WORK AT BAY DISTRICT APPROVED

Also at the August 5, 1951 meeting, Fletcher Harding reported that he was presently negotiating with Dr. Custer concerning the establishment of Second-Year College work at the Teaching Chapter in San Francisco. He proposed that Dr. Custer be nominated Regional Director of Education for the Bay District of Northern California. The scope of the Regional Director's authority and geographical jurisdiction was to be defined later. The motion was seconded and unanimously carried.[27]

SCIENCE OF MIND MAGAZINE PRICE INCREASES

At the November 29, 1951 meeting, a motion was made and carried that the price of the *Science of Mind* magazine be increased to 35¢ per copy and that a proportionate increase in the annual subscription rate be made as soon as the Magazine Department could properly effect the change. Also, Hearst

Publications was contacted with regard to possible newsstand distribution of the magazine, and it was recommended that the monthly print run of the magazine be increased by 10,000 each month. A vote was not taken.[28]

INSTITUTE AND IARSC TO SHARE REPRESENTATIVE BOARD MEMBERS

Also at the November 29 meeting, it was reported that the Representative Council of the IARSC had recommended that there be two members from the Institute Board appointed for the IARSC Council, and in return two members from the IARSC Representative Council sit in on meetings of the Institute Board. The matter was discussed, but no action was taken at this meeting.[29]

DEAN OF THE INSTITUTE ESTABLISHED, HOLMES ELECTED

The November 29 meeting also included the election of Holmes to the newly created position of Dean of the Institute:

> [A] motion [made] by Mr. [Arion] Lewis and seconded by Mr. Newell and carried, that the position of Dean of the Institute be established as the highest ecclesiastical office of this organization and that the position be filled by Ernest Holmes who is hereby elected to the position for the period of his natural life and that the salary be not less than $10,000 (ten thousand dollars) per year payable as long as he shall live with privilege granting him to retire at any time he may choose on full salary.[30]

HOLMES SPEAKS TO REPRESENTATIVE COUNCIL ABOUT HIS CONCERNS

At the December 10, 1951 Representative Council (IARSC) meeting, Holmes addressed some of his concerns regarding potential divisions:

> Dr. Holmes spoke at length, calling attention to some of the factors which had entered our movement, and which, unless checked, would tend to divide our common unity. Speaking rather freely and directly, he called attention to the fact that the Council must make a more determined attempt to [seek a] common basis of operation with the Institute in spreading Religious Science.[31]

At a subsequent meeting, Fostinis presented an item of unfinished business: a proposal made by Dr. Custer at a previous meeting in which he had made some suggestions designed to unify the functions of both the Institute and the IARSC. The Council rejected Custer's proposal, saying, ". . . it does not seem to fit into the pattern of our movement at this time. It is rejected as untimely and impractical. Mr. Spruit is instructed to inform Dr. Custer of this position in such a way as to not hurt his feelings."

The following is a recollection from a minister (Dr. Frank Richelieu) who, while attending a conference with his wife, met Dr. Holmes in a memorable encounter:

We were all attending a conference in San Diego. I got out of my car with my wife and he was in front of us, but getting out of his car at the same time. He [Dr. Holmes] said, "Hello." Now he's talking to us, my wife and me, as we are climbing up the steps to the hotel. Ernest said, "What do you think I should talk about tonight?" I was too shocked to answer. He's asking me? I thought maybe it was just conversation. I said, "Spirit will direct you and what you have to say." That's the Ernest Holmes I remember. He relied on Law and Principle for everything.

Ernest Holmes said in his talk that evening, "I turned it over to the universe. You have to direct it. The Law needs direction. Well, whatever happens is going to be right action. You create it. They [students] don't get that. No, they don't. I could go to my car, sit in my car, and say, "All right, take me where I'm supposed to go." Maybe that day will come. But right now, you'd better start it. You'd better know where you want to go. That's our teaching, kind of what I mean about the misunderstanding of Science. Isn't it a privilege? And every generation, maybe that generation needed the pioneers and maybe now what is taking place becomes more respectable perhaps, or more digestible, that people could accept it more. And maybe it is right."[32]

· 1952 ·

At the February 28, 1952 meeting of the Institute, Arion Lewis recommended that the following resolution concerning reciprocal participation of representatives of the IARSC as Institute Board members, be approved:

Be it resolved that the Institute of Religious Science join in a reciprocal policy with the International Association of Religious Science Churches under which the Board of Trustees of the Institute of Religious Science will elect to its membership two candidates from the membership of the Representative Council of IARSC which have been recommended to the Board of Trustees by action of the Representative Council of IARSC.

Be it further resolved that we recommend to the IARSC that they elect to their Representative Counsel two candidates from the Board of Trustees of the Institute of Religious Science, which candidates have been recommended through the IARSC to the Board of Trustees of the Institute of Religious Science, and

Be it further resolved that the Secretary be and is hereby directed to communicate by letter the sense of this resolution and statement of policy to the IARSC. Mr. Harding seconded and the motion carried.

Mr. Atwood appointed the following standing nominating committee and asked them to report this time as to candidates to be considered for membership. Mr. Lewis reported that Mr. Jack Fostinis and Rev. Lora Holman had been suggested as candidates for membership on this [the Institute's] Board from the IARSC and recommended that they be elected. Dr. Harding recommended that the report of the Nominating Committee be accepted and that the Secretary be instructed to cast a unanimous ballot for election for these two candidates. Seconded by Armor, motion carried.

Mr. Lewis moved that the action of the Nominating Committee heretofore, taken in recommending to IARSC Mr. Atwood and Mr. Harding as candidates for the two positions on the Representative Council of the IARSC, be notified and approved. Motion was carried.

Conclusion: Mr. Jack Fostinis and Rev. Lora Holman will sit on the Institute Board as representatives from IARSC and Mr. Atwood and Dr. Harding will sit on the IARSC Representative Council as representatives of the Institute Board.[33]

Another important matter discussed in the February 28 meeting was the ongoing negotiations to rent the Wiltern Theater. A letter was written to Warner Brothers Studios, the owner of the building, contemplating continued use of the Wiltern Theater, beginning April 6, 1952, at a rental of $200 per Sunday. Hours of occupancy were to be from 8:00 A.M. (or 9:00 A.M.) to 11:45 A.M. each Sunday; all steps previously taken by the administration in furtherance of this were authorized, ratified, and approved. This motion carried.[34]

UPTOWN CHURCH CHOIR TO BE ON TELEVISION OR RADIO

Dr. Hornaday reported in the February 28 meeting that the choir of his church would sing for the first time on Sunday, March 9, and that the Radio Corporation of America (RCA) representatives had been at his services and were contemplating presenting it on television or radio at no charge to the Institute; he asked that the Board approve the matter. Arion Lewis stated that it was the policy of the Board that any and all public worship services be broadcast by radio or television whenever it could be accomplished without cost to the Institute or further action.[35]

At the March 27, 1952 meeting, because Holmes had requested that some clarification be made regarding his permanent trusteeship, it was proposed, under the heading "Article IX: Adoption Amendment and Repeal of Bylaws,"

That the bylaws of this Corporation, except Sections 1, 2, and 3 of Article II of these Bylaws, may be adopted, amended, or repealed by the vote or written consent of the majority of all of the members of the Board of Trustees then in office. That during the tenure of Ernest S. Holmes as Permanent Trustee, Sections 1, 2, and 3 of Article II of these Bylaws cannot be changed, altered, or amended except upon his affirmative vote or written consent. Resolution passed.[36]

HORNADAY MOVES HIS SERVICE TO WILTERN THEATER

Dr. Hornaday announced that he would be holding services at the Wiltern Theater on Easter Sunday, April 6, 1952, at 10:30 A.M., and that they would be televised by KTLA, Channel 7.

Numerous amendments and bylaws changes along with a church organizational plan were being made at this time. A committee was created to work on the subject of "individual membership."

NEW DOCTORATE RECOGNITIONS GIVEN

At the May 22, 1952 meeting, it was suggested that honorary doctorate recognitions be conferred on Rev. Sally Chaffee, Rev. Ethel Barnhart, and Rev. William H. D. Hornaday. That suggestion was acted on. Also, Dr. Harding moved for the adoption of the following resolution: "Be it resolved that in addition to the present recognition 'Doctor of Religious Science' (R.Sc.D.) given by the Institute of Religious Science, that provision is hereby made to give honorary recognition in non-ecclesiastical instances as 'Doctor of Humanities' (L.H.D.)."[37] The motion was carried.

The first person on whom the board wanted to confer the degree of Doctor of Humanities was Norman P. Van Valkenburgh, President of the Institute.

DR. CUSTER AND SAN FRANCISCO TEACHING CHARTER QUESTIONED

Harding made a trip to San Francisco to meet with Custer and Rev. Wayne Kintner with regard to the proposed curriculum of the educational program of the San Francisco Church of Religious Science. It evidently did not conform to the approved curriculum. At the September 25, 1952 meeting, a resolution was therefore made:

Whereas it has been brought to the attention of the Board of Trustees . . . that the San Francisco Church of Religious Science has discontinued teaching the prescribed curriculum of the Institute, now,

Therefore, be it resolved that a hearing be had before the Board of Trustees at a meeting to be held Thursday evening October 23, 1952 at 7:30 P.M. for the purpose of determining whether the Teaching Charter heretofore issued to the San Francisco Church of Religious Science should be rescinded or revoked on the grounds that the same is not being exercised by the recent failure to offer courses of instruction as prescribed by the Institute and,

Be it further resolved that notice of the time, place, and purpose of said hearing be given to the San Francisco Church of Religious Science by mailing to the Board of Trustees of said church and to Rev. Dan Custer, minister and director of said church, a true copy of this resolution. Signed and carried.[38]

Dr. Custer sent a letter to the Board of the Institute in reply to the letter sent to him on September 26, 1952, requesting that he appear at the October 23 meeting. A letter was also read from the San Francisco Church board in reply to the letter from the Institute Board of September 26. Harding recommended that the Board suspend the teaching charter of the San Francisco Church until such time as they amended their curriculum to conform to that of the College. After discussion, the motion was duly made and carried to postpone indefinitely any action on the San Francisco teaching charter.[39]

[Editor's note: Dan Custer was a very well-known and popular minister and teacher.]

At the November 20, 1952 meeting, Rev. Holman, a representative from IARSC to the Board of the Institute, reported that plans were under way to hold an IARSC summer youth camp program somewhere in the mountains, and perhaps to conduct an adult program some time later.[40]

Hornaday reported that a beautiful pageant would be given at the Wilshire Ebell Theatre on Christmas Eve, with professional performers and Institute ministers participating, as well as the choir. Lewis suggested that the script of the pageant, written by Hornaday, be sent to the Library of Congress for copyright protection. Hornaday also reported that the choir would present a concert at the Ambassador Hotel on Tuesday evening, having been chosen to present a one-and-a-quarter-hour program at 7:30 P.M.[41]

· 1953 ·

At the IARSC meeting of January 4, 1953, Hornaday presented a list of twenty delegates and alternates to represent the Los Angeles Church of Religious Science for the IARSC Congress, and moved the board approve the list, with himself as the twenty-first delegate, and that the delegation operate under the unit rule in voting at the Congress. The motion was seconded and discussed. Then, Holman presented a substitute motion that the delegates and alternates recommended by Hornaday be elected to serve as delegates at the Congress. That motion carried. After that, another motion was made regarding the delegates' voting under the unit rule. That did not pass.[42]

THE BOARD OF REGENTS IS FORMED

The January 15 Congress of the IARSC was held in the Institute building except for the evening of the banquet, which was at the Ebell Theatre. The IARSC donated $200 to the Institute for the use of the building.

At the January 16, 1953 Board meeting, there was a motion to amend the bylaws so that the Board of Regents could be formed:

A motion was made and carried that the Bylaws of the Institute be amended to provide for the creation of a Board of Regents of the College of Religious Science composed of nine members, seven of whom would be chosen by the Board of Trustees of the Institute to serve for terms of five years with the provision that the IARSC-selected members of the Board of Regents may hold office at the pleasure of the office of the Representative Council of IARSC and that,

As an adjunct to that Board, an Advisory Committee of not less than five persons be chosen by the Board of Regents from the personnel of member churches of IARSC subject to the approval of the Board of Trustees of the Institute to assist the Board of Regents in connection with the Leadership Course.

Also that the Bylaws of the Institute shall be amended so as to delegate to the Board of Regents full and complete responsibility for the administration of the educational program of the Institute, subject always, however, to the condition that all expenditures of Institute funds be made only out of appropriation previously approved and allowed by the Board of Trustees of the Institute. Motion carried.[43]

An additional motion was made and carried that the positions on the Board of Regents for the first term would be Hornaday, Haughey, Fostinis, Armor, Holmes, Lewis, and E. J. Scanlan. It was suggested that Henry McLean of Santa Monica and Robert Bitzer of Hollywood be recommended as members of the Board of Regents to represent the field, and that Helen Heichert act as secretary. Hornaday was appointed as temporary Chairman of the Board of Regents. A motion was made and carried that Lewis prepare and present at the next meeting such an amendment of the Institute bylaws necessary to effect these resolutions.[44]

SAN FRANCISCO TEACHING CHARTER IS REVOKED

In March 1953, the final decision was made that the teaching charter of the San Francisco First Chapter [Church of Religious Science] was to be revoked. It was decided that because the classes were not those specified by the Institute of Religious Science, the teaching charter would be revoked.

GLOBAL GROUPS

In South Africa, Religious Science was being taught by Hester Brunt. She reported that a teacher could not incorporate and have a church charter with the IARSC, in conformity with the IARSC bylaws, because in South Africa an act of Parliament was required for the organization of a church. A motion was made that a teaching charter be issued to this group after the Credential Department investigated the situation, and in its opinion recommended that special consideration be given the group by the Board of Regents. The motion was carried. Auguste Berg had gone to France to translate the Textbook into French; he had assigned to the Institute $10,000 worth of stock. The money was to be used for the expansion of Religious Science work in France. In Germany, a Mrs. Krup was translating some of Holmes's books into German. And in Canada, Henrietta Lewis had a Religious Science ministry in Montreal.

CHURCH BUYS STOCK

The price of $2,500,000 was authorized to be paid as set forth in a purchase agreement for the purchase of the Hugh H. Eby Corporation of Philadelphia. The relevant resolution follows:

Whereas this Corporation [the Institute] has been presented with an opportunity to purchase all of the capital stock of Hugh H. Eby, Inc. of Philadelphia, Pennsylvania for a total sum of $2,500,000 . . . on an installment basis as set forth in a written purchase agreement dated November 23, 1953, and which said agreement fully sets forth the price, terms and conditions of said purchase, and,

Whereas contemporaneously therewith, this Corporation may enter into a lease agreement covering the assets of Hugh H. Eby, Inc. to be so acquired as set forth in the written form of lease presented at this meeting and it appears that said purchase and leasing will be in the best interest for this Corporation;

Now, therefore, be it resolved that this Corporation shall purchase all of the capital stock of Hugh H. Eby, Inc. of Philadelphia, Pennsylvania for the sum of $2,500,000 . . . as set forth in the purchase agreement dated November 23, 1953, and that contemporaneously therewith or as soon thereafter as practical, this Corporation shall enter into a written lease agreement with the new corporation to be formed, and

That the President and Secretary or Assistant Secretary of this Corporation be and are hereby authorized and directed for and on behalf of this Corporation, and Arion Lewis, Jr. as Trustee is hereby authorized and directed for and on behalf of this Corporation, to execute said stock purchase agreement and written lease and to execute for and on behalf of this Corporation any and all of the documents that may be required to fully consummate said transactions including any amendments thereof. The resolution was seconded and carried.

WILLIAM LYNN JOINS THE INSTITUTE

Bill Lynn arrived on the scene in the summer of 1953. He was readily advanced and soon became the business manager for the Institute.

I remember one time when Elmer Gifford looked at me and said, "Bill, you are probably the safest person in the organization because nobody else would have your job." (There was a bit of unrest in the organization.) He said, "The ministers don't want your job, and if you're smart, you don't want theirs."

The outside income did allow us to acquire a number of adjacent properties. When I first came to work there in 1953, the property consisted of 3251 W 6th Street, the old Institute building and a corner lot at 6th and Berendo, which was a vacant lot. Somewhere along the line, the Institute was getting too far in debt to Ernest, and they sold the corner vacant property at 6th and Berendo. A short time later, we bought it back. Some time in 1953—I can't remember the exact date—the three-story professional building between the lot and the Institute was for sale. We had the money so we bought that. Soon after that, the building immediately next to the Institute became available to purchase. It was an L-shaped building and there was a funny little three- to four-room building wedged in there. We acquired that and put the magazine department in there. That gave us full command of half of the whole block of 6th Street. . . . I was very instrumental in acquiring those two properties. The property in the back was a parking lot and behind that was an old building . . . it had been a church at one time and during World War II, it had been converted to apartments. When we bought it, it was efficiency apartments. We then had acquired roughly three-quarters of that square block. We rented that building for an apartment house for a number of years. Then we remodeled it for Sunday school and education. We had that property up until the late 1980s, when Institute management started thinking in terms of building a new building. The property, as I recall, was worth several million dollars.[45]

SPECIAL MEETING HELD TO CHANGE CORPORATE NAME

A special meeting in Dr. Holmes's office on December 4, 1953 was reported:

Trustee Lewis moved that the necessary resolution and other documents be prepared to change the name "Institute of Religious Science" to "Church of Religious Science," to be submitted for final action as soon as the necessary documents are ready for transmission to the Board. Motion was seconded and carried.

Mr. Lewis explained a proposition to purchase all of capital stock of the Oregon–Nevada–California Fast Freight, Inc. and moved for adoption of the following resolution: "Be it resolved that the offer to purchase all of the capital stock of the Oregon–Nevada–California Fast Freight, Incorporated be accepted and that the President and Secretary be authorized and directed to execute on behalf of this Corporation any and all papers necessary to consummate said transaction subject to final approval of the terms thereof by this Corporation's attorney." The motion was seconded, and all trustees present voted in favor of resolution.[46]

INSTITUTE PREPARATION FOR THE 1954 CONGRESS

At the December 29, 1953 meeting, there was discussion concerning the delegates to the 1954 Congress; a list was approved. Lewis then informed the Board that according to recent federal legislation, it would be necessary that delegates sign a "loyalty oath" that they were not nor ever had been members of the Communist Party. Fostinis was advised to prepare the necessary papers.[47]

GLOBAL REPORT

Also at the December 29 meeting, a global report was given: During the past year, the *Home Study Extension Course* in Science of Mind of the Institute of Religious Science enjoyed a large enrollment of 580 students. In addition to the United States, there were students in the following foreign countries: Canada, Australia, the Bahamas, Scotland, the Philippines, Japan, Nigeria, South Africa, and the British West Indies. There were several people taking the course who resided in Puerto Rico and Kuwait, and three or four students in the Armed Forces in Vietnam. In recent years, the Institute had enrolled students in Holland, Haiti, the Republic of Panama, Hong Kong, South America, and Mexico. Their ages ranged from eighteen to eighty-six.[48]

NAME CHANGE TO CHURCH OF RELIGIOUS SCIENCE

At the December 29 Board meeting, it was decided and resolved that the name of the corporation was and should be "Church of Religious Science." For several years, the Institute had been using the name "Church of Religious Science." Now they were incorporating under that name. At this meeting, the existing trustees—Holmes, Haughey, and Armor—met and agreed to change the name to "Church of Religious Science" from "Institute of Religious Science and Philosophy." The motion, seconded by Holmes, carried. Lewis stated that he had secured signatures of all other persons present that night for the consent of Trustee members to change the name. All nine members voted in favor. This unanimously changed the name of the corporation to "Church of Religious Science." The Institute of Religious Science and Philosophy would thereafter be an inactive corporation, remaining, however, in the organization's control. Thus, there were now two corporations, one called "Church" and one called "Institute"; the names had been reversed. It was the consensus of opinion that as soon as possible, necessary steps be taken to place the functions of the Education Department and College under the name of the "Institute of Religious Science."[49]

[Editor's note: In November 1957, an additional corporation was formed and named for possible future use: "United Church of Religious Science." For this, there was a three-member board: Armor, Gene E. Clark, and an attorney, which was approved by Dr. Holmes.]

Also at the December 29 meeting,

> It was moved to repeal all existing bylaws of the Corporation from 1935 [of the Institute] to the present time. During discussion, Mr. Fostinis and Mr. Lewis explained the new code of bylaws. Mr. Lewis moved to adopt the resolution, seconded by Haughey. No votes

were made by Armor and Fostinis. Holmes's vote was included. The other six Trustees voted in favor, so the motion was carried. After further discussion, Mr. Lewis moved for a reconsideration of the motion. It was seconded and carried unanimously. There were a few changes made, after which Mr. Lewis moved for the adoption. All members voted in favor.

Mr. Lewis also reported that the Eby Corporation purchase was completed and that in about three years we should realize about one-half million dollars. Mr. Scanlan requested that time be given at the next meeting for him to present the financial structure.

PART II: 1954–1955

We cannot grasp the meaning of Infinite Consciousness nor fathom Its depths, but we argue from the known to the unknown, from our own minds with their intelligent consciousness, to an Absolute Intelligence, which interspheres everything and is manifest through everything—this Absolute Intelligence is the First Cause or that by which everything is made manifest.

Ernest Holmes, *Ebell Lectures*[50]

· 1954 ·

At the January 6, 1954 meeting of the Representative Council [Editor's note: The "Representative Council" and the "Board of Directors" are one and the same, and the names are interchangeable. This Council held meetings separately but during the week of the Annual Congress.] of the IARSC, those present were Lora Holman, Raymond Barker, Jack Fostinis, Irma Glen, Fred Sykes, Robert Bitzer, Earl Barnum [Editor's note: In many different sources, in both official and unofficial documents, Earl's last name is spelled "Barnum" but also appears as "Barnham." For many years, he appeared in the "Directory of Religious Science Practitioners" as "Earl Barnum," and under the assumption that he would have had it corrected there were it an error, throughout this book, he will be referred to as "Earl Barnum" even where official meeting minutes and other sources refer to him as "Earl Barnham."], John Hefferlin, Cora Mayo, Jesse Longe, Ethel Barnhart, Armor, Holmes, Carmelita Trowbridge, and Iris Turk. [Editor's note: This is not the full convention of delegates.] There was a property agreement made with the

New York Church, the same plan is made with the Santa Anita Church, and several others: Redondo Beach, San Gabriel Valley, Long Beach, Inglewood, Denver First Church, and Denver Second Church. All churches are to receive a copy of the agreement between IARSC and the New York First Church, so they too may have a similar agreement.

A motion was made that since Fostinis had "betrayed his confidence in the Representative Council by working on the plan he presented at the opening business session at the 1954 Annual Congress, without the knowledge of the Representative Council, his appointment as Exchange Member of the Representative Council to sit on the Institute Board be rescinded, and the Institute be informed of this action by letter. Dr. Robert Bitzer made the motion . . . Three NO votes were registered by Dr. Holmes, Dr. Armor, and Dr. Glen."[51] The motion was passed, however. [Editor's note: As previously discussed, there had been an exchange member program between the Institute Board and the IARSC Board. One representative from each board sat on the other board. Fostinis was the IARSC exchange member to sit on the Institute Board.]

> At this point in the meeting, Dr. Ernest Holmes verbally tendered his resignation as a member of the Representative Council [of the IARSC] and left the meeting. Dr. W. W. Haughey verbally tendered his resignation as a member of the Representative Council.[52]

A letter was addressed to Dr. Holmes and Dr. Haughey "expressing regret on the part of the Council, and asking them to reconsider their resignations; the letter also requested that they advise [the Council] of their decisions in writing."[53] A motion was "made and carried that the agenda of the Thursday morning business meeting of the Annual Congress be revised so that anyone desiring to present ideas regarding the new plan be allowed to do so before the scheduled speakers proceeded with the program as outlined."[54]

On January 7, Executive Secretary Rev. Iris Turk tendered her resignation as Executive Secretary of the IARSC.[55] A meeting of the IARSC Representative Council was called for Friday, January 8, at 11:00 A.M. The discussion regarding the exchange of members of the two boards was temporarily tabled.[56]

On Friday, January 8, at the IARSC Representative Council meeting, there was a report given by Arion Lewis, Institute attorney, and Dr. Raymond Barker, Dr. Robert Bitzer, and Cora Mayo. Lewis suggested there be no interchange of Board members at that time. As it stood, the Institute was still a member of the IARSC. A resolution was to be passed notifying the IARSC of the Institute's withdrawal from the IARSC.[57]

After a general discussion with many people speaking about their displeasure about "the plan," namely Holman, Barker, Bitzer, John Hefferlin, and others, Ernest Holmes took the stage.

HOLMES ADDRESSES THE 1954 CONVENTION

[Editor's note: The following is the transcribed text of Dr. Holmes's talk on Friday, January 8 at the 1954 Convention following the discussion about the "Plan," that is, proposed changes within the organizations—the IARSC and the Institute, now to be called Church of Religious Science. Please remember that the words following are reproduced without editing, as they were transcribed into the records and official minutes of the Convention.]

Now friends; I'm reminded of Kippling's [sic] recessional, the shouting and the tumult cease. The Captains and the Kings depart. Still stands thine ancient sacrifice and humble and the contrite heart. I thoroughly agree with a man I do not know, who spoke last [to the Congress body]. There has been no disposition in my mind and I solely only and alone am responsible for the Plan. I think Jack Fostinas [sic] has been what they call the whipping boy, the Southerners you know, politically, I apologize to him and because I should have been [the whipping boy]. If you know me, you know I, ah, neither worship my own personality nor yours. I love us both. When Jesus said love your neighbor as yourself he did not say hate yourself and love your neighbor. Now I know you're probably tired of listening to me and I beg Lora's [President of the Board of the IARSC and Chair of the Congress] indulgence to have to sit here and listen to this. However, it is not a neurotic thought pattern which repeats itself with monotonous regularity throughout life. I think it is right that we should have had this rebuttal this morning. I wish there had been even more of it and more of it yesterday and [the] day before.[58]

[Dr. Holmes had addressed the Representative Council Board on this subject at the beginning of the week.]

This is a debate. It is a debate upon which probably and undoubtedly in my estimation hangs the survival of our organization as a unified movement. Because every member of your Representative Council to my knowledge and most of them I have talked with personally, are of the opinion that it cannot exist the way it is. The Representative Council can, but that our relationships cannot exist in spite of all of the love we have for one another and respect as Raymond Barker so [ably] pointed out and I agree with practically everything that Raymond said. In spite of all that there is something wrong with our setup or it wouldn't be here, isn't that right? . . .

I do not blame anyone for it. I would like you to know, however, that your Representative Council of fifteen members, that seven of them are not of the opinion of those who spoke this morning. Seven of them. That's almost half. They are [of] entirely different opinions as, they have the perfect right to be. I'm not saying who is right or who is wrong. They happen to have a different opinion than this present. The ones who spoke this morning and everyone's opinion should be respected because it is all sincere, it's all earnest, and it is all honest. Seven of them, ah, disagree and the other eight also disagree. That's fifteen out of the fifteen. It's unanimous.

Now what is it they disagree with? Not, I trust, ah, over each other and I don't believe over each other. I think they ah, they disagree as to the method of some way [of] unifying this movement so that it will operate. Our own Board disagrees, not with the Church Board, but with the methods whereby two Boards, each of which is supreme in its only place, but must function together with one purpose in mind; find it, ah, almost physically and intellectually and emotionally impossible to do it because they are not together. I believe it is the unanimous opinion of both Boards, of ah, this entire delegation that there should be, however it may be worked out, one final Board, but I do not like to use the word authority. I don't like that word. One time a Board as custodians for the authority of the movement itself. There is no other authority than that.

I thoroughly agree with the argument this morning, whoever may have made it, of those who are presenting an opposition to this Plan as it now is, which they have a perfect right to do and personally I'm surprised there hasn't been more opposition. I think it's rather terrific that there hasn't been more. As someone said to me yesterday, don't ah, aren't you worn out with this? I said no, it is the first time in two years I've had a sense of relief, because I know that one way or another, if your council, who are left on the Council and you as delegates desire a separate organization, I wouldn't even raise my voice against it, for two reasons: one, it would be futile, not only I do not like an argument, and ah, I would think you would have a perfect right to do that, ah, I know that that is the intention of the remaining members of your Council because they have so stated this morning. There can be no question about that. They have a perfect right to do that. A complete right to do it. I applaud their frankness in saying that that's what they intend to do. I consent that that's what they have a right to do. I do not necessarily agree that it is based on truly altruistic, impersonal, ah, opinions, because I think my being for this Plan is based on a personal opinion too. I don't know how we get away from it. I believe that it's in sincerity just as I believe in our sincerity.

The trouble with us is that right now in debate—and this is a debate—and this is a rebuttal. The trouble right now is that our whole method of procedure is "you and us" and not "we." That's our whole trouble. We have never had any other trouble. We will never avoid this trouble unless somehow one final Board, which I thoroughly agree should represent the movement. NO one disagrees about that. Has the privilege of executing the authority of the group.

Now I would like to answer first of all because I would not have Raymond think that I had been personally referring to him yesterday. I don't even know what it was I said, probably used you and Bob (Bitzer) as an example an illustration. God knows there was nothing personal since you're very close friends of [mine]. I mean, ah, if ah, if Raymond wasn't a close friend of [mine] he and I wouldn't have written a book together that's just published. We hadn't sent that to publish and then each get out our razor and go at each other like, ah, I understand the coward man, the war was going over the top. Well, when the bugle came he threw down his gun and his knapsack and grabbed out a razor and slashed at a Hun and the Hun said, Huh You never touched me. This man was pretty wise, he said just wait until you shake your head. You see, it was a complete cut. Now, that is in all honesty and fairness if we desire a clean cut. If your present members of your Board desire that, let's have it. If the members of our Board desired a complete severance of this Institute from the church, let's have it. I don't think either one does. That is my opinion.

Now, I would like to mention about the surprise with which the Plan was introduced. Let me ask you this—several hundred people come together here in convention at one spot for the first time in a year, everything that's been proposed by everyone here has been a surprise to everyone who came from the viewpoint of the one thing proposed, hasn't it been? I mean, let's be rational about these things. Is it or is it not a surprise? I don't even know who's going to be nominated. A convention is full of surprises because everyone gets up and introduces an idea. Suddenly it's a surprise, but it could not be any other way nor is any new proposition anything other than a surprise. That takes care of that.

Now the next that the [IARSC] Board were ignorant of this Plan. I ah, I'm not saying they were not ignorant. I am merely saying this, so far as I know they were individually acquainted with the Plan, or had the privilege of becoming acquainted. I talked with Lora about it for an hour and a half. She said I don't know whether it's good. She said if it is good I would like to see it go over. If it isn't, I wouldn't. That's obvious. She said, I will not oppose it, well, she has a perfect right to oppose it, and if the majority of the people want it I'll go along with it. That's fair enough. I ah, wrote to Raymond Barker and told him what I knew about it; Jack did and he said he thought it was good; I ah, talked to most of them and they thought it was good. So it does not come as a surprise either to the individual members of the Board; I invited two or three to come who didn't come. I cannot be responsible for that. It is not a surprise, either to the individual members of the Board or the other.

This is a Plan that can be adopted neither by our Board or your Board that ah, for the field. It can only be adopted by the members of the field. Now, I would like to come now to the next idea because you see, we all say that we like the Plan but we don't like the way it's put together. That's true, isn't it? I mean the opposition does. Maybe it's put together wrong. I'm not saying it's a perfect document. I don't expect it is. But remember this, I did not come before you and say you will take this Plan or leave it . . .[59]

[At this point, there was an exchange between Ernest and several members present. The following is the exchange as it appears in the Convention records, with speakers identified as they are in the records.]

Several voices: *Yes, you did . . . yes sir . . . yes you did.*

Holmes: *I did?*

Other voice: *You did.*

Holmes: *I, I think you misunderstood me.*

Other voice: *No.*

Holmes: *Now, I'm willing to be misunderstood; I'm willing to have said it if I did. If I said it then I will say that I said it. I'm not trying to avoid that issue, you understand.*

Other voice: *Ah, Ernest, Mr. Lewis just said it, now I don't think you need to change it.*

Holmes: *Yes, well, I'm not talking about that . . .*

Other voice: *Yes, Mr. Lewis just said it . . .*[60]

[After this exchange, Ernest continued speaking for some time; his words continue next.]

I ah, this Plan is not presented to you as ah, something that you as individuals have to except [sic]. I have been aware for two years and have continuously warned individual members of our Board that ah, they, the setup would lead to some kind of separation if ah, the separation took place, that separation would lead to another separation and that one to another one cuz I've watched it in similar organizations. It always does that. Finally we would have nothing. That's pretty liable to be it you know. That's the way those things happen. New [sic] it became very evident to me a year ago that something definite would have to be done. Last summer I determined to do it, to introduce some know [sic] of an idea that would put the thing together. This is the idea. It came up out of ah, necessity. It came up out of the knowledge that we were not functioning in harmony and in unity; but this discord isn't a discord as we think of it a disunity as we think of people fighting each other, it wasn't that at all, or disliking or hating each other, nothing like that. It's a disunity that grows out of the division of a final, ah, place of agreement where the authority of the movement is represented by the movement.

And so this Plan has evolved out of it and now let us think about the democrative [sic] side of it and maybe it isn't democrative. If it isn't, I don't want it . . . at all. Ah, I only believe in the democratic process. Now let us consider whether or whether not it is democratic. Ah, you see, you are

*going to be the judges, I'm not. I'm not trying now to say believe me and
don't believe anyone else. I'm merely pointing out the facts as I see them.
This Plan may or may not be democratic. Let us look into it and see and
let us also consider, is it as democratic as under the present situation it is
possible to make. I'd like to bring that alternative and not as something
that you should have to accept but as something that I suggest, merely. In
the first place, out of nineteen members, the field would appoint seven. I'd
like to get back to the permanent Trusteeship first. That is undemocratic.
I have never said it wasn't. Ah, Mr. Lewis, our attorney, has always said
it was, he's never been for it. Jack Fostinas [sic] wasn't for it. Most of my
Board have not been for it. This is a strange situation, isn't it?*

*Well, I just happen to be a purpose, a person who for twenty-five years
has had only one purpose in mind. And I have known that until that
purpose was accomplished within the possibility of such ability as I have,
if I live, that purpose cannot be clouded by, by anyone. I may be a hundred
percent wrong, but let me tell you this; the institutions of this world that
have survived and brought forth civilization are the lengthened shadow
of certain definite thoughts. I say that impersonally. It is most certainly
true. You can take the best thought and the best idea in the world and so
twist it and reinterpret it that it loses its entire validity and effectiveness.
I'm not saying my ideas are intolerable, I'm just saying I am aware of that.
You all are aware of that. Therefore, I have not and do not intend, this is a
notice to Mr. Lewis as well as to you, to give up my permanent trusteeship
in the interest of Religious Science. (Applause) Until and as such time if I
live, the purpose for which it exists, that I may not myself be thrown out
by someone who doesn't know what that purpose is. (Applause) That's
what I believe. Now that's undemocratic. No one knows it any better than
I do. That's autocratic. That's 100% arbitrary. I stand before you and tell
you this; that if it hadn't been carried out, we wouldn't be here, if it is not
continued to be carried out I would bet ten to one that my own Board
would destroy it; yet I love them. Then you might say: "well, what a guy
you are, what a guy. Cicero is dead and Caesar is dead and I'll be damned
if you feel well yourself." That's what you'd say. (Laughter from the floor) I
can only say, I can only say, in the terms of Mark Anthony not that I love
Caesar less but, that I love Rome more.*

Let me tell you something my friends, you do not know what life has been for twenty seven years. You haven't the slightest concept. It's creating something out of nothing. It's financing that is keeping it going when Boards come and leave and get mad and go away and take their own, and have every legal and moral and ethical right apparently to think it; and you trust yourself when all men doubt you, but make allowance for that doubting for no great thing has ever happened to this world unless there was such an idea behind it, and never will, because gradually to it will be gathered those who'll agree with it because they will see. I have no visions, no dis—no special dispensations of providence, God hasn't touched me on the should[er] and said "Ernest, tell them this and make it stick." I don't believe in that.

You have all agreed that we have very good teaching. It is not my teaching. I have too much of a sense of humor to come before you and say I content for my [a blank line in the minutes reflects an unintelligible phrase here.] If what we teach is not true, the greatest thought of the ages is false. Whether it be psychological, scientific, mystical, metaphysical, philosophical, or intuitional; if what we have is not true the greatest thought of the ages is false. But the application of that will continuously change. This is why I provide that all of my writings go to a movement. To what movement? One that's divided against itself? Not at all. That too will be torn to shreds.

I propose to continue with that persistent and consistent program until there is unity; if I am living; until there is solidarity, if I am living; and that which guarantees such intelligence as I've had, and I am not a fool, that it will continue. If that happened tomorrow I should give up not only my permanent trusteeship; I should resign from every Board, retire from all public activities as I now conduct it and give myself the privilege only of speaking for such members of this group as would wish me to just for the joy of doing it. I could not think of anything that would make me as happy as that. I certainly hope that something will be worked out so that that can take place. I wish again to return to this idea of the permanent trusteeship. Dr. Hefferlin knows that his permanent trusteeship is not democratic. He's a smart man.[61]

[Ernest directed comments at this time to several members present, and the exchange is recorded in the following.]

Holmes: *Bob (Bitzer) knows his isn't—don't you Bob?*

Bitzer: *Sure.*

Holmes: *Carmelita [Trowbridge] knows that hers isn't. She's a smart woman.*

Bitzer: *But I don't have a world movement—I have a church . . .*[62]

[After "much discussion from the floor," Ernest continued.]

Ah, Ah. Now wait a minute . . . [everyone was talking at once . . .] Now, now, now wait a minute. Now wait a minute. Now let's wait a minute. A principle is true wherever it works, wherever it works. (Applause) You're in the world movement Bob [Bitzer], just much as I am, just as much as we are. That's one of our troubles. I've got this; you've got that; we have this; they have that. We all recognize this. Alright, the permanent trusteeship is autocratic. I cannot help it. I cannot help it. I thought long and earnestly when members of my own Board have labored much harder than you have to get rid of me in my capacity. Don't think that I haven't. The most strenuous opposition I ever had was [Arion] Lewis, he's still at it. But I'll say one thing, he's right out on top about it. He's always honest. I don't think he's always right, particularly about this. Jack [Fostinis] does not believe in the permanent trusteeship. Bill Hoy does not believe in the permanent trusteeship. The President of our Board, Mr. van Valkenburg does not believe in the permanent trusteeship; and neither do I, but I shall continue in it. (Laughter from the floor) I have no other prerogative. The very fact my friends that this argument comes up here this week and came out of a necessity, a definite necessity which all of us agree to; is a definite sign that the time at least has not yet come to make that change. I wish it had, more than all of you unitedly could wish. Well, now let us see about whether or not the Plan is democratic. First of all, let me say this please, cuz this is the last time I shall ever speak to you on this subject. It is possible that this is the last time that I shall ever speak to the Association of Religious Science Churches [IARSC] . . .[63]

[The tape ended here, and the transcription of Ernest's comments picks back up in the following.]

. . . I hope not. I would like to read this with you because you alone decide. I don't. Your Board doesn't; our Board does not. You alone decide and decide individually. I presume there are certain features about this Plan that are not democratic.

Now, the only feature that I can see about it that wouldn't be is the division on the Board. That's right, isn't it? I can't right now think of any other, any other thing, it is certain that we are not trying to give a system of laws and orders to somebody. If we were; if our method were arbitrary, now maybe the Plan is undemocratic but the method is not arbitrary. If the method were arbitrary we would have simply announced we have a Plan, take it or leave it, don't even read it, don't even try to decide whether you like it or not. Nobody's done that, nobody['s] done that at all. I said yesterday because it was proposed at the last meeting I attended as a member of the International Association [IARSC]. I'm no longer a member of it. Dr. Bitzer said I would be returning the whole thing [IARSC] back to the Institution. I said, Bob, I wouldn't accept it. I wouldn't either.

There is no one here who wishes arbitrarily to go over anybody and I don't know how they could. In the first place, every church owns its own property. They are a member only by their own sufferance. The group elects seven members to our Board; I, if that's the only point that I can see that we have a difference of opinion on. I don't believe that there's any legitimate, ah, reason, for any other difference of opinion because the Plan itself, as such, ah, part of which you haven't read, is a complete revision of our own constitution bylaws to adapt itself to such a federated movement, such a unified movement, perhaps I should say. The Plan calls for just what we have. It had been my idea that the Board of [the IARSC] Representative Council of which I then was a member would continue to function just as it was. They collect the dues or whatever you want to call them, the per capita membership, they spend it, for the ecclesiastical purpose; [it's all right]. They, they are repre—they are elected by the field.

Our Board of Regents, it was mentioned this morning that our Educational Program has been rather chaotic. Well, I wouldn't say that. It hasn't been bad. But this last year as you know from the field of the Institute there has been appointed or elected, I don't know how it was brought about, I am on it but I never go to it, because I don't think I know anything about it. A Board of Regents, Bob [Bitzer] is one of them, ah, to decide what our curriculum shall be and work it into something that shall be your guide. I think that's democratic. Seven members are to be chosen from our field who help to elect the other twelve members. Their votes are just as valid as anyone's. Now here is a point that I'm willing to debate with you. I'm only too glad to concede your point and have no desire to evade or avoid the issue. That isn't good debate. That isn't good intelligence. It's intellectual dishonesty too. I just don't know of any other way to do it.

Remember this: this is a move that inevitably passes what I have, what I have done, what ah, we possess into a world movement. It's the first move that's ever been made to do it. It's made deliberately. It's made dispassionately. It's made calmly. I will go so far as to say that it's made with a hundred percent of intelligence. It's made honestly in knowing what we're doing. I would not know of any other way to do it. Now this is my opinion. I would be willing. I think it will take a number of years to effect such a change.

Personally, I will be willing that periodically at the [end of a period] of five years another one were elected by the field, in another five years another one, and another five years another one. Now I cannot speak with ah, authority I'm telling you what I would be willing [to do]. Now we bring this Plan to you. I bring it to you really and I trust that you will not criticize Mr. Arian or Mr. Lewis or our Board. [I] trust your whole criticism, any condemnation or judgements that you have will be directed to me because I know so well how not to take it. You see, I have an umbrella and enjoy the moisture of the rain. It keeps one's skin from drying.

Now, I alone am responsible. I want you to know this and I would like that to stay. It looks as though we ought to have twelve members of one and twelve of the other. Our experience of the last few years has taught us that I, I don't think for a few years it would work. I may be wrong. We, I believe that's the only point of contention, however.

It is not legitimate that you say the Plan is sprung on you. That's not legitimate. It's so evidently not true. It is not legitimate that it has been sprung on your Board. They have all been told about it and knew about it and ah, seven out of eight out of fifteen are for it. So that isn't legitimate. That's not an argument. That has no validity. It is not true that anyone is trying to push a Plan down your throats because they couldn't. This is an individual thing with you and with your church. I would be willing to debate it with any church membership who wanted to know about it, be willing to go and tell them. On the other hand, now I am speaking from our position. Your position is just as valid as mine.

We asked you to take the plan home with you and submit it to your board. Most of you are going to do it, apparently from having signed a requisition. Now, in your signing that, you are not saying you are going to adopt the plan. You're not even saying your church will adopt it. You know whether you will adopt it—I don't. You cannot know what your church will think about it. The members, of course, have to decide. Perhaps they will entirely reject it. That's alright. It's your right to oppose the plan. I do not even know if that plan will go on; you see, we haven't come and said, you have to accept our plan. Not at all. All that we have said—and now may I say, all that I have said because we, in this case unfortunately is I . . . I know it's wrong, but having admitted my, I trust that I shall be forgiven. I shall forgive myself anyway; and there is no other forgiveness. (Applause) I am growingly aware that much of our condemnation of others is that we can only see ourselves wherever we look. It's always that way. It's never different.

The plan that I am asking, now, then: I'm not just saying take it home and accept it or go out of business. I'm not saying like me or don't like me. There is no such thing as that; nothing of the kind. In all that you decide to reject, I shall only be affected in that I shall be sorry. That's what we're asking: that you take this plan that we presented with much thought, which *has much in it that's desirable, and perhaps much of it is undesirable, and give it your consideration. We have no other privilege. We have no other desire. I am willing that there should be a logical, sequential, periodic . . . Jesse Longe spoke to me about this the other day. I'm willing that that should be; it seems to me that would be logical. I believe that right now I'm going to say to you: you elect twelve, we'll have twelve. I will be the deciding one, because I have no intention of quitting what I started. That's out. I mean, if that's wrong, it remains wrong. I can't help it. You'd be in the same position. I should always decide what I think is in favor of the field. The field is the church.*

I would be perfectly willing—and I'm speaking only for myself, for such a periodic change. I think it's logical. I think it's intelligent. I think it's rational. I know that Jack or Arion would agree with that, but I would be willing to bet that they would—wouldn't you, Arion?[64]

[At this point, there is an exchange among Arion Lewis, Ernest Holmes, and Jack Addington.]

Lewis: *I think that inevitably it's an evolutionary process.*

Holmes: *That's what I mean.*

Lewis: *It should be stated by formula in advance that there would be an advantage in so doing.*

Holmes: *Yes, I believe that. Now, I believe if you would have understood this, you would have maybe felt a little differently about it; but I don't know.*

Addington: *I'm all for the unity, Ernest.*

Holmes: *I know you are, Jack.*

Addington: *. . . basic idea of the plan, I believe, though, I don't like to see this situation where you have eight on one side and seven on another. I don't like to see schisms.*

Holmes: *Well, I don't either, Jack, I don't, now . . .*

Addington: *I believe we should get together.*

Holmes: *I do. I, I'm just say[ing] this now. We are all agreed to that. It may have looked at times—I'm very sorry to take so much of your time. . . . Are you indignant because I take so much of your time? ("No's" from the audience) Please, please do not leave . . .*

Holman: *Will you excuse me just a minute. I think, it's 12:00 and almost time for us to adjourn and I think the Election Committee should proceed.*

Other voice: *I think this is more important.*

Holmes: *Ah, well that's quite alright.*

Holman: *Yes, but we do have other things.*

Other voice: *But this is more important.*[65]

[After this exchange, Ernest Holmes continued once more (following).]

If that's what you wish to do. I will not take much more of your time. And realizing the seriousness of the situation as I do better than any of you, I cannot say that I have more at stake than any of you because I have nothing at stake personally. The world has given me everything that it gives to most people and more, of pleasure and happiness and love and friendship and contentment and intense activity which is life to me.

I believe ah, being a student of history which I read continuously that there are the deepest plantings in this world are never harvested by those who make them on earth. They never have been; they never will be. If they were they would be shallow and something would uproot them. I believe that they will be harvested somewhere else. Therefore, I would desire that if we harvest, we would all be glad to reap wherever we may be and I sincerely believe that. I am a long-term person, perhaps with a vision, perhaps not.

I am so aware that today, this hour, this moment, so totally aware, so dynamically aware that this hour decides the fate of this movement. It does, my friends. I face it without trepidation or fear. I have only relief at the thought that no longer shall we go on as a house divided against itself with nobody to blame. . . . I would say "we" are wrong in the way we have put something together. I would be perfectly willing, as I say, periodically for this change. Of course there will be suggestions about this Plan when you've read it. Remember, you are not accepting this Plan. No one has asked you to accept this Plan. No one would think of asking you to accept this Plan.

You have merely been asked, will you receive it in your hands; will you be gracious, tolerant, considerate—and kind enough to take it home and go over it yourself because there's about 50 pages of it; and with your Board; and present it to your membership and see what they think of it. In all probability many of these groups will say we would accept it but we think there are certain things that would be good with it. That's inevitable. This won't be accepted tomorrow or the next day. I don't believe it can be done in 30 days. It maybe will take a year to completely accept or reject it—that I do not know. I do not think that time is of the essence of the agreement here. It is intention and purpose and accomplishment is the essence of this agreement—isn't it? Don't you feel that way, Jack?"[66]

[Jack Addington responded to Holmes, next.]

Addington: *Well, I feel this way Ernest, ah, that ah, it would be very difficult to go back to a membership and to then ah, just as here, the membership would say, well, what's going to happen? You don't have anything centered and it's the easiest way. I mean, the whole thing, the IARSC then, ah, it would lose the push behind it because people wouldn't know which way to go.*

[After some additional comments back and forth, Dr. Bitzer and Dr. Holmes had the following exchange.]

Bitzer: *Well I, I just feel that ah, the people should know that ah, four of the members of the Representative Council who are, are for the Plan are all members of the Institute.*

Holmes: *That's right, that's right.*

Bitzer: *That leaves only three members from the field, presuming as it, at the ah, membership has been poled [sic], because I do not know how it's staying. Ah, one of those ah, three from the field would represent the Representative Council member who for the past months has spent most of his time with the Board of Trustees at the Institute in working out the Plan.*

Holmes: *That's right.*

Bitzer: *So as far as I know, that only leaves two members that you might say strictly from the field, ah, are for it and I'm working on the assumption that one of those members ah, is the member of a church ah, at which the Permanent Trustee is for the IARSC. So I, I don't, don't think it ah, the people, should feel—*

Holmes: *That's right.*

Bitzer: *. . . that the Council have been canvased [sic] and then poled [sic] because we have not and ah, we're assuming that they don't know—*

Holmes: *Well, ah, I'm glad to make this correction Bob, if it is a correction, ah, that's alright. I thought, I thought that seven members of the Board were for it and eight I do not know what they're for. I still think that seven members of the Board of the IARSC are for the Plan. I still think there are eight that I do not know what they think and it isn't any of my business. I'm not questioning the integrity of the intelligence of their conviction what, at all, now, . . . please Paula, I hate to do this but—*[67]

[At this point, Paula responds, "I think you have done enough talking . . ." and the record indicates that the tape ends. When a new tape begins, Ernest is speaking again, in the following.]

Let me just conclude my remark before we do that. It may be that you'll completely reject the Plan. It may be you will completely accept the Plan. It may be that the idea of getting together can be accomplished even though you take the Plan for consideration—I mean there is no document that is infallible. There is no group of people who should be so arbitrary as to say 'we alone know the truth'. But I would like you to feel this—on what might be the last occasion except tonight, when all this will be over with. I mean tonight we meet in festivity, in, in something else. I would like you to feel the sincerity of it, the humility of it. I would like you [to] feel that for thirty years and more, someone has had one vision—someone who knows the pitfalls better than any of the rest of you, and I would like to tell you this because this I know—unless some Plan is adopted whereby we may function as one the first thing you know you'll be functioning as twenty. I hope it may be avoided. I pray it may be avoided. I believe that it will be avoided.

There are many heartaches even in religious organizations if you've had very much experience you know them. One is a target for public approval or disapproval. His motives are somewhat suspected. There is nothing more nor should there be anything less than an honest, sincere person can do than to trust himself. To seek such wise council as he knows and has and is obtainable and go ahead that way. I sincerely believe, for the last time I shall ever mention it, that with the possibility of the exception of a periodical switch, now, I don't believe in saying only all you understanding, I believe that this Plan could so cement this movement together you see, it isn't arbitrary.

Raymond Barker, you all have a, a school in your own church. No one interferes with you. You have an international Board [the IARSC] to work it out. No one here interferes with them. Ah the, the course in Leadership Raymond Barker is going to give and Stan Bachness this next year it will be begin[ning] in San Francisco if our group were ready for it but, they are giving you the other course.

It's a pretty universal plan so I just say this to you my friends, quite dispassionately, more dispassionately than at any other time because I have nothing, believe me, but a sense of relief about this. I know it's going one way or the other. I know is better than you do. I knew it when I started it. But I will say this; let us hope, and as Paula said, pray, that if you are wrong something will happen, if we are wrong something will happen that IT may be right. It's bigger than we are.

We have worked, we have labored. We have had successes and failures together. We have suffered and rejoined together. And should we part, let it be in peace. Should be [sic] remain united as is my ah, permanent desire, my prayer and yours in this garden of our mutual endeavor let us walk together then in that garden fearless heart not apart, for they who know the joys and sorrows of their lives have known cannot walk alone. (Applause)[68]

[Jack Addington was next recognized by the Chair, and he and Ernest Holmes had a brief exchange.]

Addington: *Thank you Lora. I want to make my position clear. The other day when I spoke, I spoke in behalf of unity. I'm still thinking about unity, but there are a couple of questions I would like to ask. I talked about the Plan and I talked about the possibility of a change, of compromise to this Plan. Now I would like to ask Dr. Holmes a question and it's a yes or no question. Would the Institute of Religious Science, Board of Trustees, be will[ing] to sit down with the representatives of this group and work out a plan that is acceptable to everyone along the lines that they have suggested? I was told that that was a skeleton. I was asked for suggestions. I had no way of knowing what the people would want. They said it was a skeleton plan, you'll fill out the details later. Now I'm all for unity. I'm for Dr. Holmes, I'm for Lora and for everybody because we're all together in one but would the Board of Trustees of the Institute be willing to come to compromises where we will all fit into this thing? Does that, could we Ernest?*

Holmes: *I know of no reason why they would not.*

Addington: *Well do you think they would?*

Holmes: *I know of know [sic] reason why they would not, Jack.*[69]

At this point, Dr. Holmes yielded the floor and left the meeting. He turned and walked down the stairs. [Editor's note: This account was corroborated to me by Dr. Raymond Charles Barker and Dr. Carlton Whitehead, who were present.]

COMMENTS ON THE CONVENTION AND "THE PLAN"

The following is from an interview with Dr. Frank Richelieu conducted in 2011.

Something very interesting: When the split came, that was the hardest thing for Ernest Holmes to see. Ernest Holmes was a member of the IARSC, and he withdrew from the IARSC, and the other churches made the choice to remain or to stay. Carmelita Trowbridge made a statement when he passed away, "Dr. Holmes died of a broken heart. To see what you created and all of a sudden there is dissension, which Ernest Holmes treats with love and harmony."

I'll never forget, Ernest Holmes, we were walking, and he put his arm around my shoulder and he said, "Do you believe that you can teach this?"

And I said, "Yes."

"Do you believe in absolute treatment?"

"One hundred percent."

He said, "Why don't you go out and start your work?" I'll never forget what he said next: "It's the consciousness of the minister that is the success of the church. It's the consciousness of the minister that is the failure of the church." That stayed with me.[70]

CHURCH OF RELIGIOUS SCIENCE MEETS AFTER THE CONVENTION

Mr. Chamberlain of the Board moved that the Church of Religious Science organization resign from any relationship with the IARSC, seconded by Arion Lewis. The motion carried.[71] Concerning Church teaching charters, Lewis suggested that any and all teaching charters granted by the Board of Trustees or the Board of Regents to any church that did not affiliate with the Church of Religious Science under Chapter 5 of their bylaws be revoked and withdrawn at the expiration of the current enrollment commitments that had been made, and that each church so affected be immediately notified not to enter into any enrollment commitments after February 28, 1954. This motion was also carried.[72]

It was also decided at the January meeting that the Department of Executive Administration would be directed to advise each IARSC church that had not made application for affiliate relationship that the listing of their church would not in the future be carried in the *Science of Mind* magazine, and that any reference to IARSC would be deleted from the magazine as soon as possible.[73] Holmes stated his desire that each church listing be carried until it was definitely known that a given church was not associated with the Institute and the Church of Religious Science.[74]

At the same meeting, the following resolution to change the bylaws was made:

Be it resolved that Section 5, Article 7, Chapter 1 of the bylaws of this Corporation is hereby amended to read as follows: "Privileges of Licentiate Ministers: A Licentiate Minister shall be entitled to exercise and to enjoy all the rights and privileges of a minister except to the extent that the civil laws of any state or country may restrict the exercises of such rights and privileges within its jurisdiction, subject however, to such limitations that may be imposed by specific grants of such recognition." Passed.

IARSC MEETS AFTER THE CONVENTION

A special Congress of the IARSC was called for May 20 and 21, 1954, to be held in Long Beach, California, at which Dr. Barker announced:

> It is the purpose of this Congress to go ahead and not back. It is the purpose of this Congress to discuss the present and the future but not the past . . . Jacob wrestled all night with an angel. The decision was I will not let thee go until thou bless me. We are releasing the past with our blessings. The wrestling is over . . . and we are like Jacob . . . we are given a new name. You will remember that God named him Israel. He with whom God hath prevailed—We have wrestled. Your Council has wrestled. The wrestling is over and we are accepting for this organization, [its] Council and every [church] the wisdom that God has prevailed and everybody is in their right place doing their right work.[75]

The council then continued with the business necessary to move forward after the recently initiated reorganization.

> The next order of business was the introduction of new council members who had been selected to fill the unexpired terms of members who had resigned. Dr. Barker called the names individually, told whom they were replacing and the length of their term in office. The new council members were as [follows]: Dr. Victor York Briggs, Mr. R. Terrence Moore, Mr. Leonard Fillmore and Mr. E. C. Jameson.
>
> Motion was made and carried that these council members be approved by the Congress to fill the unexpired terms of members whom they replaced. . . .
>
> Dr. Cora B. Mayo was called to present the revised I.A.R.S.C. By-Laws made necessary by the re-incorporation of the I.A.R.S.C. It was moved that . . . all amendments to the By-Laws, as presented

to the Congress, be considered at this time and if accepted be prepared by the By-Laws Committee and inserted in their proper order in the By-Laws. . . .

[It was moved that] the first amendment regarding the Ministerial Alliance of the I.A.R.S.C. [read] as follows: Be it resolved that the International Association of Religious Science Churches organize an "International Religious Science Ministerial Alliance" as a department of the I.A.R.S.C. All ordained ministers of Religious Science who are members of the I.A.R.S.C. in good standing are eligible for membership. This organization to elect its own officers, set up its own By-Laws in harmony with those of the I.A.R.S.C. . . . be accepted and thereby become a working structure of the By-Laws of the I.A.R.S.C. . . .

All licensed Practitioners who are members of a Religious Science Church, which is a member in good standing of the I.A.R.S.C. and/or practitioners who meet requirements prescribed by the By-Laws of the League, shall be eligible for membership.

Religious Science Churches shall appoint a Board of Regents to prepare a complete course of study in Religious Science, Science of Mind, and related subjects through the facilities of the College of Religious Science incorporated in Colorado; . . . all recognition for classes completed shall be granted by the Colorado Corporation . . . Each individual Church of Religious Science through its Board of Trustees may secure permission to teach these courses in its own modality, but no degrees or recognitions shall be issued except by the Colorado Corporation.[76]

In the same meeting, Jack Addington requested an "Amendment 4," changing the name "Representative Council of the I.A.R.S.C." to the "Board of Directors," and the IARSC accepted resignations from the following churches: North Hollywood, Oakland, Santa Monica, Oklahoma City, Pomona, Denver First Church, San Francisco, West Valley, San Fernando, Ventura, Honolulu, Burbank, Whittier, Seattle, Boise, Richmond, and Riverside, as well as the Monrovia and Fullerton study groups.[77]

At this time, the IARSC was beginning to create its own Sunday school (called "new church school") materials, financial reports, insurance, and all necessary items for organization.

· 1955 ·

CHURCH OF RELIGIOUS SCIENCE BUSINESS MEETING

At the 1955 Annual Convention of the Church of Religious Science, a business meeting to discuss and resolve many different matters was held. After the opening meditation and a few brief words from Dr. Holmes, Van Valkenburgh stated, "The organization is in better financial state than it has ever been and . . . it will continue to grow financially and metaphysically as a whole as well as in the individual organizational committee, churches and groups." There were ninety-nine delegates representing forty-two churches present.[78]

Churches wanted help in particular methods of financial structure. To help fulfill this request, a person from headquarters would go to the churches and help them establish their financial structure to fill certain needs. Rev. Warren Burtis, who was very familiar with accounting, said that he had a system of bookkeeping or accounting which he had just learned; while many pastors call themselves bookkeepers, he said, there is a difference. He had a simple method to which he had changed from the double-entry system, and he was saving himself, he said, eight to ten hours a month.[79]

The president of the Board was Jack Fostinis. He explained that there was to be a Nominating Committee. The duties of this committee were to decide on and present to the Convention the names of the nominees for the specific offices to be filled. There were seven offices to be filled on the Board of Trustees and twelve on the Church Council. At the 1954 Congress, the Church Council members were elected to serve until the end of 1954. The term of office for the members of both the Board of Trustees and the Church Council was three years, one-third of whom were elected each year. At this time, they needed people to serve both bodies for periods of one, two, and three years, each office being numbered according to the bylaws.[80]

On the Church Council, position number one was filled by a nominee selected by the Board of Trustees; Dr. Hornaday filled this position for 1954. The other twelve portfolios were filled by election. In this body, the offices were numbered and each had a particular function. The bylaws provided that a committee was to be appointed at the first business session of the Convention and was to report at the next session. This report was to include specific names for specific offices. In these nominations, consideration was to be given to particular qualifications of the people chosen. The committee expressed appreciation of any suggestions from the delegates.[81]

A report by Dr. Stanley Bartlett of the Education Committee said, "The tuition price levels are satisfactory and expansion is expected."[82] He also said that there should be an *earned* doctorate, as suggested by some; honorary doctorates were given out, perhaps too freely. For an earned doctorate, a course with paid tuition should be added to the curriculum. There should be a tuition paid, but attendance would not be necessary in a formal class. Perhaps they would present a thesis of 15,000 words. This proposition was to be submitted to the ministers, then the Church Council, and in turn to the Board of Regents for their consideration. At one time in the past, the Institute had an earned doctorate, but there had been many problems with it. In the event that this time the idea was accepted, the Committee recommended that it be carried out as outlined.[83]

In Denver, both the master's and bachelor's courses were being conducted, with about one hundred students in the college work there. The curriculum was always the problem, because people required different courses of study. Some had had formal education and were good students. Some were very religiously minded and had come from orthodox church work. Their approach was more "mystical." Many were nonreligious and had no religious background. These people were more likely to require a psychological approach to study. There was, then, the problem of bringing all these classifications together. The approach to the problem was to try to coordinate the mystical and psychological. Study was required so that the teaching might be advanced by breaking down the master's course into specialized training units rather than having a few lectures on various subjects. The Education Committee recommended that this matter be studied and a revision of the master's course be undertaken with the idea of reducing the overall schedule of teaching to certain specific group studies for specialized training.[84]

Another problem was that the first-year work comprised 120 hours. Should it be strictly Textbook work, or should it include the Bible and psychology? It seemed to the Education Committee that it would be good to concentrate on the Textbook, with emphasis on teaching the students on how to do treatment. It was estimated that only about 5 percent knew how to do treatment after taking the first-year course. If that was not accomplished in the first year, there had to something wrong with the teaching work. No matter what else the curriculum included, students had to be taught to do treatment.[85]

For pre-church study material, it was recommended that people use the *Home Study Course*, the *Revised Home Study Course*, or other courses used that were based on books: *The Science of Mind, This Thing Called You, This Thing Called Life*, or other Religious Science books similar in nature and value. This alone would eliminate confusion.[86]

Irma Glen, Music Director, was a world-renowned musician and organist. She provided hymns and recorded soloists for conferences and individual churches. She had arranged for the Temple Record Company to make a record for the Church. This company dealt mostly with prestige records and records that were collector's items. She lectured on the healing philosophy of music. She composed music for the Youth in Truth movement, and she arranged for the Church's hymns to be released through ASCAP, which was good for prestige, and she compiled a list of the people, musicians, and singers, who believed in the Church's philosophy and wanted to work in the field. Her recommendation was to give the record and hymnal to radio stations in the various localities of affiliated churches.[87] [Editor's note: I don't know if this took place, nor the result of such a program.] Glen closed her report with these words: "Divine philosophy and music are my life. Music is intangible and, more than the other arts, most closely approaches divinity. In music, each one responds according to what he brings to music. Religious Science is creating a new musical literature."[88]

Ethel Barnhart gave the Ethics and Consciousness Committee report. She did not have a written report, but stated that a manual for the field needed to be very complete and coordinated. She went on to say,

There is a story about a schoolteacher that I would like to share with you. At Christmas time, she was talking about the shepherds and the wise men. After the story, she told the children to show her what the story had meant to them by drawing stories. Most of the children were drawing scenes of the manger and the wise men and the star of the East. But the teacher came to one boy who had drawn an airplane with four people in it. Three of the people had great shafts of light around them, but the fourth did not. When the teacher asked the boy how this was the story of Christmas he explained that the three people with light were the wise men, and the fourth was Pontius the pilot.

We now have in Religious Science more than a philosophy. Ours is the teaching of the Christ way of living, of knowing one's Oneness with God and practicing this. We should get the human ego out of the way long enough to practice. What we know, we should practice. Part of the new cycle is to become more aware of what the teaching embraces so that Christ can give us light and guide each one of us. Something will flow from each of us—the Spirit that moves the words, for the words themselves are only the vehicle. We have something new to do. We must find a new awareness within ourselves. We say the same things so often that we lose the fire and are deadened. It is necessary for us to be quickened within ourselves—each one of us. There has been much prayer work done for the movement during these past months and it is bearing fruit. It shows on the faces of the people.

In the realm of outer things, services have been prepared for your use and have been given to the Church Council office. In preparing the services, we have kept in mind that every service should reveal an inner truth. The service itself is only the structure through which spirit moves. The service is merely to represent that something which is to be given in a particular area. The power of the living Spirit must move through the service.[89]

The Sunday School Administration report was given by Dr. Willa Fogel:

Since Ernest called me many months ago to serve in this capacity, I have written over 260,000 words of finished manuscript and more than 2 million words in rewrite. This represents between 1,500 and 1,800 hours of work. All of the material is completely new. Those of us on the committee have worked so hard because we knew that we were formulating the material for our Junior Church. We have been developing a three-year Bible course with interpretation according to Religious Science.

We are using progressive methods and are working on the basis of four age levels. For each thirteen-week period there are five manuals in addition to one Teacher's Manual for each age level. There is a Superintendent's Manual. This contains each Bible story written in full plus outlines for special programs such as Christmas and Easter. These two special programs, plus the candle-lighting ceremony and outlines to be used in the assembly, are contributed by Phil Gatch. The teachers have the lessons for the age level with which they are working. The Bible story starts the theme. Each level is repeated every three years but in a different way so that monotony will not be a factor to keep the children away. Also in the Teacher's Manual are suggestions for activities. There are pictures for each lesson which carry out the theme.

> Mabel Leonard is our Activities Chairman. Our Work Materials Chairman is Ethel Lloyd. An Evaluation Committee analyzes and makes suggestions about the manual material which I submit to them. This committee consists of the Chairman of our various subcommittees and one or two others.[90]

On Wednesday morning, January 5, 1955, the Congress continued with the Ministerial Placement Committee Report given by Elmer Gifford. He and the committee had placed six ministers during the year: Rev. Dodson in Big Bear, Rev. Bryson in Pomona, Rev. Moen in Hemet, Rev. Iverson in Fullerton, Rev. Cantrell in Santa Rosa, and Rev. Merrill in San Francisco. In each of these cases, he went to the Board of Trustees of the churches beforehand to find out the needs of the locality. All of these people were doing a good job. The Ministerial Placement Committee duties included placement of ministers and assignment of speakers to substitute for ministers who were away for any reason. There were speakers who were traded around quite a bit. This gave students a chance to speak before various congregations.[91]

The Budget Committee Report was given by Rev. Harold Hull. The information was from the Comptroller, Mr. Russell. In 1954, there had been income of $6,729.20, and total expenses of $9,175.25. This showed a loss of $2,446.05; however, there was anticipated additional income for 1954 of $2,200, which would make the anticipated net loss for 1954 only $246.05. "We feel that this is a good closing picture for the first year of the new beginning," said Rev. Hull, "especially when we consider the loss of churches that did not affiliate."[92] The proposed Church Council budget for 1955, which would be submitted to the Board of Trustees, included $31,600 in expenses.[93]

Dr. Hornaday gave the Board of Regents report:

> I would like to explain to you who come from a long distance that the Board of Regents have jurisdiction over only the First and Second Year work and the Practitioner's Clinic. During this convention we have heard some excellent recommendations for the people who have talked to us and I would invite all of you to leave with us, in writing, such recommendations. The Board of Regents is made up of people in the field who are teaching this work as well as those who are here. All of your suggestions will be read. We welcome suggestions regarding the curriculum. Those of you from the north, from out-of-state, or in practitioner's work will have especially valuable suggestions. I am chairman of the Board and have called this meeting together since we are

about to have our election. I want to thank all of you who have cooperated so beautifully, for after all, it is your Board of Regents and your college course. It is only as we work together that we will do our best.[94]

The Youth Activities report was given by Norman Lunde, chairman. He gave the following report:

At the seminar they had seventy young people attending. They all had a great deal of fun and held regular meetings. During the year, much has been done in individual groups, for example, the Alhambra Group organized the first baseball team in Religious Science. They treated for their team and for their playing and, incidentally, won the championship their first year together. The Headquarters Group, Los Angeles, has square dances two Saturday nights a month for fun and fellowship. At the Snow Ball, which was held just before Christmas, there were about three hundred young people present. The band leader told me that they all behaved in a wonderful way and they had quite a jam session too. One boy said that any church that can throw a wing ding like that was good enough for him. It has generally been the case that those youngsters who most need Religious Science do not attend the group activities. It is good to have those with problems and even with police records with us so that we can teach them and help them with their problems. After all, our purpose in Religious Science is to reach all the young people we can and to teach them love. We had our first convention Sunday of this week and there were 150 youth delegates in attendance. Last year when we held our first meeting, there were 40 delegates present. Many ministers complained that they have no young people in their churches. It amazes me that they restrict their vision in this way. The very thing that started the church itself can start the youth group. The manual after three months of planning is ready and I would like to suggest that each of you ministers pick up one of these whether you have a youth group at present or not.

The chairman of the Club Activities Committee, Dr. Mabel Kinney, gave the following report: "I just had a call from the office of the Governor in Sacramento. The message was that a measure was submitted to the legislature yesterday by G. D. Morris proposing that the taxes on church parking lots be abolished. Do I have your consent to follow through on this? From your reaction I guess I may assume a yes answer."[95] Since Dr. Kinney's report was available for general distribution, only an outline of her speech was included in the minutes. She discussed beatitudes for club groups, factors in effective club organizations, questions and Dr. Kinney's answers, Korean students sponsored by the Women's Club, the Women's Guild of the First Church of Los Angeles, distribution of the "Prayer for Universal Peace," and a conclusion: "Divine agreement is the Law of the Kingdom and we pray that we may work together and our club will be the hub of this activity. The theme that we suggest for next year is found in the following question: 'What does the Lord require of thee but to do justice, to love kindness, and to walk humbly with thy God?' "[96]

The closing meditation for the meeting of the 1955 Church of Religious Science Annual Convention was given by Rev. Orrin Moen. [Editor's note: It seems that each year the Annual Convention was called something different. It was called the "Church of Religious Science," "Affiliated Churches of Religious Science Annual Convention," "Convention of Religious Science Churches," and most often the "Annual Convention, Church of Religious Science."]

CORRESPONDENCE FROM CECIL B. DEMILLE

A letter dated July 23, 1955 to Holmes from Cecil B. DeMille, the celebrated movie director, reads: "Dear Dr. Holmes, thank you for the autographed copy of your book, *Words that Heal Today* which Mr. [Donald] Curtis brought to me. I am particularly interested in the way you treat the 'Lord's Prayer' in Chapter 7, pausing to meditate on each phrase and thus drawing deeply on the inexhaustible meaning of that great prayer." [Editor's note: Cecil B. DeMille directed the classic film *The Ten Commandments*, which featured Donald Curtis, who was for many years a Religious Science minister. Curtis later moved to Texas as a Unity minister.]

At a special Finance Committee meeting on November 1, in preparation for the 1956 Congress, it was recommended that first, a definite plan for the greater use and distribution for the self-supporting services, college, and magazine by the church and their members be put into action at once; second, that the Board take immediate and necessary action to put before the 1956 Congress a per capita increase in dues from $2 to $5 per year, per member. If worthwhile, the Board might suggest to the churches that this additional assessment, or all of their assessments, might be raised by some special fund-raising activity.

THE FIRST ISSUE OF THE RELIGIOUS SCIENCE MAGAZINE

The first issue of *Religious Science* magazine, published by the IARSC, was dated December 1954, and titled *Daily Word for Effective Living*; the cost was 25 cents. [Editor's note: The magazine would later be named *Creative Thought*.] The size was 5 ¼ by 4 inches. The inside cover reads:

> Your daily pocket guide. This new magazine is an additional channel for Truth. It replaces none and enhances all. It is streamlined, compact and direct. It will fill the need of busy people who desire a pocket full of Spiritual ideas to make easy their day. The action of God takes place through these pages and all who read them will be permanently improved. Truth reveals itself through ready minds and the open heart. God, the one Mind, is both the writer and the reader. Divine Ideas are its only activity.

The magazine includes some one-page articles and thirty-one days of meditations. The back cover reads, "International Association of Religious Science Churches, Dr. Raymond Charles Barker, President, Headquarters, 624 S. Virgil Avenue, Los Angeles 5, California."

Also given in the back of the magazine under "Who's Who in This Issue": Dr. Raymond Charles Barker, New York; Lora Holman, Glendale; Paul Brunet, New York; and Robert Bitzer, President INTA, Church of Religious Science, Hollywood.

After that is a directory of all churches. Twenty churches are listed, including one in South Africa, Hester Brunt, minister. This is followed by a list of practitioners by state then city, with one practitioner listed for the British West Indies. [Editor's note: By June 1955, there were twenty-seven churches listed in the magazine, then titled *Creative Thought*, including one each in Calgary, B.C., Canada; London, England (Miss Marjorie Raven); and South Africa.]

A special article by Raymond Charles Barker is titled "What You Believe Happens":

> We believe in one Universal Spirit manifesting through all nature and incarnated in all men.
>
> We believe that the Universal Spirit is personal to and reveals itself through everyone who recognizes its presence.

We believe that our faith operates upon a Law of Mind which automatically manifests in our experience according to that faith.

PART III: 1956–1959

The genius of the new Science of Spirit, which is destined to save the world, is its direct approach to God and its conscious use of God Power in every activity of living.

Ernest Holmes, *This Thing Called Life*[97]

Bill Lynn was business manager of the Church of Religious Science at the time, and he related the following in an interview in 2011:

During the time I was there [at the Institute], the organization went from a very shaky financial position [in the 1950s], a period of wanting to leap ahead and wanting to grow and not quite enough money to do it. We moved into a period of business. Somebody came to us, I don't remember the details, it was a long time ago. At that time, we had several businesses that were brought to the organization and it was a matter of taking advantage of the tax structure of the time.

And during this time, mid-1950s, and it went on for a number of years, the earnings from these businesses were what enabled the church to get out of debt. One of the first things they did was pay off Ernest. Ernest had kept the church afloat out of his own pocket. I remember when one of the first big checks that came in from the outside earnings, the church wrote a check to Ernest. I want to say it was probably close to $100,000; I can't remember the exact amount. I remember they delivered the check to Ernest, and Ernest gave me the privilege of going over to the Ambassador Branch of Bank of America where he had his personal account, and deposit the check. That was when the church was finally out of debt to Ernest. He had met the payroll for two or three years, and a number of other things. That was when growth started taking place. That enabled us to start building Founder's Church. Contrary to what some people like to believe, the congregation did not build Founder's Church. The unrelated business income did.

There wasn't universal agreement as to whether the church should be involved in these businesses. A lot of the ministers did not think we should be involved.

[I asked Bill, "Was there any problem with the IRS in this regard?" He responded:]

No. Everything that was done, as far as I know, was totally within the law. We had good counsel, and the church turned down a number of proposals. The tax laws changed. The IRS did away with non-profits having income. I was the director at the time, and I liquidated the last of the businesses, Standard Wire and Cable.[98]

At the January 16, 1956 meeting of the IARSC Board of Directors, a conversation regarding the right to use the name "Church of Religious Science" was held:

Dr. [Raymond Charles] Barker explained the legal technicality involved when the names of two corporations were transferred and they are now legally incorporated under the name "Church of Religious Science."

It was then discussed how best to notify the I.A.R.S.C. churches of the tactics of "divide and concur" being used in the various churches so that they may be prepared to meet the situation should it infiltrate their church. After much discussion it was decided that Dr. Barker send out, as soon as possible, a "State of the Union," letter regarding the I.A.R.S.C. to all leaders and ministers. It was also suggested that this letter be published in every I.A.R.S.C. church bulletin. This was asked for in a motion so the following was made and carried: that the president, Dr. Barker, should write a letter to the churches in as brief form as possible, setting forth the accomplishments of the past year, reaffirming our progress and asking the ministers to print it, if possible, in their monthly bulletins or send it out in some other way; that we pay no attention to the Institute; that we move forward in faith and determination and that [evil] of itself will die of its own weight if not recognized. So, let's move forward with love and faith and determination. Wherever the President thinks it necessary to inform anyone he will do it by personal letter.[99]

THE IARSC: WHAT HAPPENED NEXT

At the March 12, 1956 IARSC Board of Directors meeting—one year after the "split"—Dr. Barker read a letter from Dr. Hester Brunt of Cape Town, South Africa, "wherein she stated that she had managed to get the Articles of Incorporation and the By-Laws of the Chapter completed. With approval of the Board, they would be known and incorporated as the First Church of Religious Science, Science of Mind, of Cape Town, South Africa."[100]

At the September 6, 1956 meeting of the IARSC Executive Committee, Dr. Carlton Whitehead, minister of the Monterey, California church "was asked to explain the action regarding the 1957 Seminar [possible meeting at Asilomar]. Dr. Whitehead stated that he had been negotiating with officials of Asilomar, California in regard to holding the I.A.R.S.C. 1957 Seminar there in August of that year. Dr. Whitehead further stated that Asilomar had given him a definite time limit to notify them whether or not this was an actual agreement."[101] After discussion in the committee, the following motion was made and carried: "That the I.A.R.S.C. 1957 Seminar would be held at Asilomar and Dr. Whitehead be empowered to notify Asilomar—by long-distance phone from Coronado—that this was a definite agreement."[102]

THE YOUTH OF IARSC

At the November 12, 1956 IARSC Board of Directors meeting, Dr. Robert Bitzer reported that he had visited the teenagers' seminar held in Idyllwild, California on the weekend of November 9. Dr. Bitzer praised the organization highly, as well as the program carried out by the teenagers' group. He gave a brief synopsis of the program that had been scheduled. Dr. Barker stated that should this seminar for teenagers continue in the future, it should have some authority by the IARSC or an IARSC church behind it.[103]

This led into a lengthy discussion regarding legal responsibilities, youth committees, and young people's councils to confer with the IARSC Board on activities of this kind.

> Following discussion, this motion was made and seconded:
>
> That this body appoint a youth committee to keep in touch with just such activities. Dr. Bitzer spoke to the motion suggesting that a top level conference for youth groups be held to discuss the youth activities. Others spoke to this idea, bringing out that we had already appointed a youth committee. It was noted that the

functions of the present active youth committee did not include activities of this kind. The above motion was withdrawn and a new motion was made which read:

That we set up a teen-age committee to work with the I.A.R.S.C. on all future activities. . . . After still further discussion the motion was withdrawn.

A motion was made and seconded that we appoint a teen-age committee of the I.A.R.S.C. composed of adults who are interested in teen-age work, and some teen-agers; the proportions to be determined by the Board at a later time.

The above motion was then restated to read: That this Board authorize the President to establish a teen-age committee of the I.A.R.S.C. composed of seven members who are to be adults interested in the teen-age activities. More discussion followed the motion when Dr. Jesse Longe suggested that the committee be compose of ministers. The motion was withdrawn again.

A motion was made that a top-level conference between teen-age workers and all Ministers shall be called by the I.A.R.S.C. to formulate plans to recommend back to this body . . . [T]he motion carried.

Dr. Barker accepted the recommendation of Dr. Bitzer and Dr. Addington to appoint Mr. Joseph Kerr as Chairman of this committee and to call the meeting at the convenience of the members on his committee. Mr. Kerr [was] to be notified of this action by the Executive Secretary of the I.A.R.S.C.[104]

PRACTITIONERS LEAGUE

At this same November 12 meeting, the subject of the Practitioners League was raised:

A letter from Dr. Margaret Bradshaw, president of the Practitioners League, was read wherein she asked for answers to the following questions:

1. At whose request was the Practitioners League organized?

2. What is its purpose other than stated in its Constitution and By-laws?

3. What is its relationship to the I.A.R.S.C.?

4. Does the Board of the I.A.R.S.C. believe the League is serving its expected purpose?

5. What do the Ministers and the Boards of the individual Churches believe the function of the League should be and accomplish?

A motion was made and carried that this letter be duplicated and copies sent to all Board members for study, [to] discuss it with their own practitioners and bring their answers before the Board again at the next meeting.

The question of holding a Practitioners League meeting once a month at the Headquarters was brought to the floor. It was clarified that this is a closed meeting for Practitioners and those intending to become Practitioners.

A motion was made and carried that pending the full study of the previous letter of request from Dr. Bradshaw that for the present time the Practitioners League be granted permission to use the facilities at the I.A.R.S.C. headquarters for their monthly meetings with the understanding that these are not open to the public.

Dr. Bradshaw gave a brief report of the activities of the League.[105]

· 1957 ·

At the January 7, 1957 Board of Directors meeting, there was a report of the vice president's tour. Dr. Addington and his wife had toured several churches to make reports. They visited Fresno, Monterey, and Palo Alto, California; Spokane, Washington; Calgary, Canada; and churches in and around Los Angeles. Addington reported that, basically, they were all doing very nicely. Some met in homes, some met in rented buildings like the YWCA. Dr. Barnum stated that he thought this was the greatest thing the IARSC had undertaken, and that more work of this type should be done. He suggested that a vote of thanks and appreciation should be given to Dr. Addington for his efforts on behalf of the IARSC.[106]

THE PASSING OF HAZEL HOLMES

On the evening of May 21, 1957, Dr. Holmes arrived home from a board meeting or class, expecting the customary warm reception of Hazel, his beloved wife of thirty years. Strangely, the house was dark. He immediately went to Hazel's dressing room, where he found her in her bedclothes on the floor. The ensuing years were difficult for him; even though he knew that life continued, there was great grief. He would live three more years until his own passing in April of 1960. Some say he died of a broken heart.

During the next three years, Dr. Holmes searched for answers, and for companionship. He invited Reginald and Elsie Armor, and Bill and Jane Lynn to come live in his home with him. Both had to decline, as they had families. Dr. George Bendall, however, accepted the invitation and spent approximately two years with Ernest in his home.

Dr. Holmes continued his speaking engagements. He believed that Florida was the closest in consciousness to California, and he wanted to start a church there. He traveled to Florida, speaking before hundreds of people, and he also taught classes. Rev. Cay Thompson's mother held a class in her home at which Ernest spoke to the students. He asked Norman Lunde to start a church in Miami. Rev. Lunde, his wife Rev. Dorothy Lunde, and daughter, Barbara, moved to Florida and started the Religious Science movement there. Barbara is now Dr. Barbara Lunde, with her church in Boca Raton.

Rev. Thompson said of Dr. Holmes:

> He was so passionate with his ideas of spreading the Truth. It felt very good. He was so amazing in his humbleness. It was just his way of being open and honest and at the same time knowing that what he was saying ... there was going to be more to it. He felt so nonjudgmental, so light.[107]

Dorothy Procopenko—younger daughter of Reginald and Elsie Armor—and her husband, Serge, would often be called by Ernest to come to his home.

> On several occasions, Ernest would call when there were small things to do around the house and around the yard in which Serge and I would help when we were first married [about 1957; Hazel had already passed on]. We were young and healthy so we were able to move furniture, hang a picture, perhaps help clean up after a party or something like that.
>
> At his home at 6th Street and Lorraine, there was an enclosed yard where there were trees and plants, and in the center there was an island area in which there was a tree and plants. Ernest was preparing for a

wedding to be performed in his yard/garden. On this occasion there wasn't any color in the yard. The yard looked lovely, the lawn was clipped. Everything was very nice but he thought we should have some color. So, we went to the store and purchased all different kinds of cut flowers. When we returned Serge and I proceeded to go around the whole yard, sticking flowers in the soil amongst the plants to bring color into the yard for the wedding.[108]

IARSC HEADQUARTERS

On September 23, 1957, a regular meeting of the IARSC was held at their headquarters building located at 212 South Western Avenue, Los Angeles, California. There was a plan to "establish a 'Master File' in the I.A.R.S.C. office which will deal with every Church and every individual, [for the purpose of having] a complete and comprehensive record of every Church or individual in any way connected with the I.A.R.S.C."[109]

At the December 2, 1957 IARSC Executive Committee meeting, there was discussion of why it would not be advisable to hold an IARSC Seminar in 1958. Dr. Addington said that the only available dates at Asilomar were in September, and it "was the consensus of the ministers that a seminar at that late date would not be feasible."[110] Dr. Addington urged that the IARSC put "all [their] energies and efforts into making the Congress in May [1958] the most successful one ever held by the I.A.R.S.C."[111]

· 1958 ·

THE HUMOR OF ERNEST HOLMES

In May of 1958, Dr. Holmes had requested that he be allowed to visit the summer camp of the IARSC in New York. He and Irma Glen took the train. In a letter to Raymond Barker, he confirmed both his arrival on June 27 at Grand Central Station and his hotel reservations in New York to be followed by the trip north to Lake Minnewaska. The last paragraph of his letter reveals his humor: "I am looking forward with a great deal of pleasure to the trip to the Lake and only hope no one tries to drown me. Of course I can always walk on the water or do something so have nothing to fear. With love, as ever, Ernest Holmes."[112]

THE ETHICS OF ERNEST HOLMES

The following letter of August 18, 1958 shows something of the ethics of Ernest Holmes:

> My dear Raymond [Barker]:
>
> Someone has sent me a list of the names and addresses of those people who attended your Lake Minnewaska Seminar. I am returning it to you since I never would take advance [sic] of such a thing to write to people or try to sell them anything—I just do not believe in doing any such thing. I have just now received the letter and opened it and am returning it to you just as I received it. I think that imposing on other people's effort is a terrible thing.
>
> At any rate I guess you are a nice guy and I like you. It has been hot as hell out here but we were all at Camp Asilomar last week and had a wonderful meeting. Everything there is wonderful except we are growing so large they cant [sic] take care of us on the grounds and we have to turn so many away. But it was still a very successful week and the camp itself is beautiful.
>
> Hope everything is one hundred percent above par with you.
>
> God bless you!
>
> Ernest Holmes[113]

Another letter to Dr. Barker from Dr. Holmes dated December 1, 1958 reads in part:

> Thanks a million for sending me the cutting about Bill Olvis.
>
> It is wonderful news. I'm glad you are changing over with Norm [Lunde]; he will be staying with me while he is here.
>
> There is no reason why we shouldn't cooperate because, somewhere along the line some people are going to come along who are smarter than you and I are and put the whole thing together. . . .

· 1959 ·

A SPECIAL RECOGNITION FOR DR. HOLMES, BUILDING FOUNDER'S CHURCH, AND HAZEL HOLMES MEMORIAL

On January 9, 1959, Dr. Roy Nichols presented the following resolution and memorials:

Be it resolved that this convention does hereby go on record as expressing its appreciation to the Board of Trustees of church headquarters for its gracious subsidy of the Department of Affiliated Churches during the past and preceding years. It is our earnest desire that the measures passed at this convention further steps up the ladder toward maturity and that the dedication of our people to the principle of sharing and the work and expense of our Department of Affiliated Churches will soon make it possible for us to become self supporting.

Be it resolved that this convention hereby voices the esteem which we and other organizations which we represent have for our beloved Dean and Founder, Ernest Holmes. Our hearts are humble in gratitude for the message he has given the world, both for the vistas of understanding he has opened to us and for the "good life" he has taught us to seek, to find, to enjoy and to share.

We deeply appreciate the work, the understanding and the love of the one who has brought to a focal point in our time the ageless truths of a diamond of many facets known as "Religious Science." We have thrilled to the news, that we have received at this convention, of the objective edifice to be built that will be known as the Founder's Church. This name is most appropriate, yet we know that as grand and as beautiful that this edifice will be, it will not equal the beauty and the simplicity of that consciousness of which the outer is but a reflection.

Dr. Holmes has stressed the fact that we have gathered truth from many sources. This fact we fully appreciate, yet we appreciate too, the further fact that truth disbursed is unrecognized and unusable. It has been the genius of Ernest Holmes that has provided the avenue through which the timeless truths can find practical application in time—our time. It is of this that we are mindful in speaking of Dr. Holmes as "Founder of Religious Science."

Yes, we thrill to the news that this idea we term "Religious Science" is to have a physical home, even as the idea has already found a home in our hearts. The physical home will be magnificent with its towers reaching upward symbolizing the upward reach of the idea of "Religious Science."

Yet, there is another tower of which we would now speak. This is the tower of strength that through many years has sustained, inspired and comforted the spirit of our founder. We speak now of our beloved Hazel Holmes who has departed from our objective view since we last met in convention. Yet, "departed" can never be the right word. She is with us still in the work that has been done and in the work that is to be done in the field of Religious Science. Jesus said, "Lay up your treasure in the kingdom of heaven." Hazel Holmes did just that. She left us rich in love, rich in understanding, and rich in the wisdom of the Father; and as the door opened outward onto a view made more beautiful through the acquisition of that inner wealth, the wealth of her love eternally moving forward remains with us, enriching our lives today. Let us resolve to go home from this convention mindful of the wealth that has become our legacy; mindful too of the responsibility placed upon us to add to the treasure that has been bequeathed us.

Be it resolved that this body hereby acknowledges that this convention has been a manifestation of dedication to Religious Science principles, which cannot be lost or swayed. Dedication is not something one deliberately seeks rather; it is more like the faith of a scientist proving a natural law. We have such dedication, not as a result of seeking it, but as a result of testing, proving, depending upon, trusting in and thoroughly loving the principles of Religious Science.

In particular we do hereby express our gratitude to all those who through their dedication have worked so graciously and diligently to make this convention an harmonious, unified and inspiring success that it has been, fully knowing that this success is the result of the combined efforts and consciousness of our convention committees and those committees and groups who have so beautifully provided the music, the floral arrangements and the ushering, our Church Council, our Board of Trustees, the headquarters staff, the participants, you the delegation and those back home whom you represent.

And, be it further resolved that we go home with grateful hearts, uplifted spirits and a broader vision of greater goals.

On January 31, the Santa Anita Church of Religious Science (IARSC), Rev. Ethel Barnhart, minister, was dedicated. On February 12, the Christ Church of Religious Science in Whittier was dedicated. Ernest Holmes was the featured speaker and reportedly had a very special experience during his talk. Some in the audience believed he went into a trance. That full talk was recorded and has been published in several books, including: *Light* and *In His Company: Ernest Holmes Remembered* by Marilyn Leo.

A BRIEF HISTORY OF THE MINISTERS OF RELIGIOUS SCIENCE LEADERSHIP

The leaders of Religious Science have always gotten together for fellowship dating back to 1927 when Dr. Ernest Holmes founded the Institute. In due course the Institute developed an Association of Chapters which later became an Affiliation of Field churches. In the 1940s a small group of ministers of the then "Chapters" of the Institute began meeting together monthly for lunch and discussion of church affairs. By the 1950's this group had grown into definite Associations of Clergy; one in Los Angeles and another in the San Francisco area.

It could be argued that it was the ministers and not the churches that formed the International Association of Religious Science Churches in 1949. Also, it was the ministers, not the churches that were involved in the "split" which occurred in 1954. It was also in 1954 when the first summer conference was held in the High Sierras. There, and at subsequent summer conferences held at Asilomar, ministers met together in workshop sessions. As an outgrowth of these summer workshop sessions it was decided to move towards an annual conference exclusively for the clergy. A committee was formed and the first such conference was planned. It was held on March 31, April 1 and 2, 1959. Dr. Craig Carter was the Chairman.

The ministers again met in Santa Barbara in 1960, but it was a somber affair as Dr. Holmes had just made his transition on April 7. "I move that at this meeting we officially constitute and establish an informal organization of Religious Science Ministers to be called United Clergy of Religious Science and it be organized in the immediate form of a nine man cabinet—that cabinet to be charged with the working out of the details of procedure; and that we consider it now so constituted." With those words in the form of a motion made by Craig Carter, and seconded by George Bendall, our present ministerial organization came into being. The motion was amended to strike "informal" and in the amended form was passed.

After many meetings and much discussion, it was moved that the post-Easter Convocation in 1964 would become independent of the Affiliated Churches of Religious Science. It took five years to be formally organized as the United Clergy of Religious Science.

In the1970s the United Clergy severed their close association to United Church and became a "loose" organization. They continued their annual convocations and locations were chosen at the invitation of a host minister. In 1979, when Ralph Tuckman was President, the tradition of helping ministers to attend convocations through grants was initiated.

In 1981, the ministers held a mini-convocation in Orange County just prior to the United Church 1981 Annual Convention. New bylaws were being written and the ministers were there to help in that process.

In 1986, the first convocation was held outside the continental United States. It was planned for Hawaii. The naysayers didn't believe that the ministers would attend because of the high cost and I suppose other reasons. However, that convocation, up until that time, was the best ever attended.[114]

In the 1980s, the spouses (wives and husbands) were invited to create their own conference to take place during the ministers' business meetings. Some spouses would attend these meetings—Marilyn Leo, Walter Reed, and many of the spouses of new ministers—while others, such as June Kelly Vogt, Marigene (Munson) DeRusha, and Harriett Henderson were a few of the "shoppers." In the early days, there were also the "poolside" spouses.

CHURCH OF RELIGIOUS SCIENCE MINISTERS' CONFERENCES BEGIN

The first formal conference of ministers took place on March 31, April 1, and April 2, 1959, at the Miramar Hotel in Santa Barbara, California. It was later planned that these conferences would take place annually, the first full week after Easter, with meetings, workshops, and free time to "relax and restore." It has become a businesspersons' association, independently incorporated, meeting each year.

At the ministers' workshop at Asilomar, in the summer of 1958, several ministers agreed that a conference just for ministers would be a desirable activity. A committee was appointed by Craig Carter, President of the Ministerial Association in Los Angeles, who was to develop a program to include time for five principal activities: (1) an hour of meditation; (2) an hour of discussion; (3) an hour of views on noncredentialed courses; (4) an hour of views on subjects of general interest; and (5) an evening period given to Dr. Ernest Holmes for lectures and questions.

At that first conference, Ernest Holmes spoke the first evening on the subject of "the mystical concept of the impersonality of the universe." Many discussions took place during the three-day conference, and of course the subject is still discussed today: "Are we a Christian church?" Ernest Holmes agreed that "we are that, and more." But, he cautioned us against stating that we are not a Christian church: "It would shock too many and you would lose a great many members." He also spoke to this subject during the Asilomar meeting in 1959.

During those early years, the spouses, mostly wives, were not invited to attend business meetings, but were invited to the opening and closing banquets. The spouses present relaxed around the pool of the hotel and went shopping, or remained at home. The second night of the conference, the spouses were invited to the banquet, which was fun for all, and Ernest Holmes spoke on mysticism. A few, just for fun, wore badges stating that they were either "Pool-Siders" or "Prayer People." There were a few ministers who joined them.

These are the final words of the minutes of this meeting: "This Conference was a *great* experience, and a *historic* one. Most fortunate are we who were part of it. As is the first 'summer camp' in the High Sierras many years ago, this Santa Barbara Conference will long be remembered. It has released into our movement a new thing . . . the suggestion that the Ministers of Religious Science should discover what is meant by 'interior life,' by 'dedication,' and by 'mysticism.' So let it be."

BOOKS PUBLISHED DURING THE 1950S

Books by Ernest Holmes published in the 1950s included: *The Creative Power of Your Thought*; *It Can Happen To You*; *Practical Application of Science of Mind*; and *The Voice Celestial*. In 1957, with Willis Kinnear, Holmes produced *The Basic Ideas of Science of Mind*. In 1955, Willis Kinnear had become the *Science of Mind* magazine editor. In this capacity, for many years, he took many of Ernest Holmes's writings and talks and published them as books. In 1974, Kinnear was named publisher of the *Science of Mind* magazine, and in 1975, he retired as Editor Emeritus.

Epilogue

Hazel Holmes's sudden death in May 1957 brought three years of deep sorrow to Ernest Holmes not previously experienced. He continued his speaking engagements across the United States, but his sadness was apparent to everyone. However, he still managed to keep his sense of humor and appreciation of life.

On the first Sunday in January 1960, the Founder's Church opened with Reginald Armor, the associate minister, conducting an early meditation/healing service, followed by Ernest Holmes giving the first service, and the church's senior minister, Dr. Hornaday, giving the second service. The opening of Founder's Church added a historic edifice to the landscape of Los Angeles. The round building was a showplace, with the main auditorium seating 1,600 people. In addition to the sanctuary, the church included Hornaday Hall, Holmes Chapel, and Armor Lounge. A painted mural by Wallace Stark was mounted behind the choir loft. It is named Wisdom of the Ages and depicts almost eighty symbols representing the whole spectrum of human knowledge and understanding throughout the ages. It appears to be a stained-glass window, but is painted, and with the proper lighting, it is a glorious work of art.

On April 7, 1960, it was time for Ernest Holmes to move on from this world—to discover if that spiral of life was truly what he had anticipated. Life as he had dreamed was becoming different at the Institute of Religious Science, now known as the Church of Religious Science. The teaching arm would continue to be called "The Institute," and the administrative arm, "Headquarters." Things were changing; not the teaching, for the students of Ernest Holmes remained steadfast to teaching what he had taught them, but the leadership and the administration were changing.

There was the constant question of who was going to take Holmes's place. Holmes did not specifically assign that role to anyone, so upon his death, there were those who had their own personal ideas of who should take the lead.

Volume 2 begins with January 1960, and through the next five and a half decades, we look at the trials, tribulations, successes, and failures that took place in both the International Association of Religious Science Churches and the Church of Religious Science. They would both soon be renamed, to Religious Science International and United Church of Religious Science, respectively. Within these two separate organizations, there were ministers who wanted to explore reuniting, as Holmes always hoped would take place, but the weight of those who did not was too heavy, and it took six more decades for that dream to come true.

During the 1970s, the International Association of Religious Science Churches changed its name to Religious Science International. The United Church of Religious Science declared that there would be 700,000 members by the year 2000. The students of Ernest Holmes were beginning to dwindle. Reginald C. Armor, close friend and colleague from the time he was twelve years old, made his transition.

In the 1980s, the United Church of Religious Science decided to hire administrative leadership from outside the church organization, expecting greater administration skills. Also, because society recognized different ways of learning among students, instructors began to change the style of teaching Science of Mind classes within the United Church. The length of classes became shorter, and teachers truncated lecture time.

During the 1990s, the last of the students of Ernest Holmes were passing on. For example, William Hornaday, senior minister and a close colleague of Holmes, made his transition in 1992. Both organizations began greater expansion of Science of Mind works around the world, and the Committee for Cooperation made progress on reunifying.

In the decade of 2000, Religious Science International established Peace Centers, and the Season for Non-Violence—a program from the Association of Global New Thought—became an annual event. Both organizations went through surveys and facilitated meetings to establish branding and name changes. In addition, both organizations embarked upon transformation in organizational processes.

The decade beginning with 2010 is our present experience, and we are growing—in awareness of the Divine, in Love and Compassion, and in the free expression of All Life.

Volume 3 will be researched and compiled when another historian steps forward, perhaps after another decade or so. No matter what evolution the Centers for Spiritual Living may experience, I believe the Science of Mind teaching will live on forever in all areas of life.

Marilyn Leo

Appendix

In this appendix are a few quotes on many subjects, taken from more than forty interviews that were not used in this volume. They are, in my opinion, very worthwhile. They are presented in alphabetical order by last name.

Awakening humanity to its spiritual magnificence.

ICSL vision statement

REV. GORDON BISHOP
Ed.D. Chaplain, semiretired, San Diego and Texas

I am very confident that as chaplains, people in our teaching can be themselves. There is no shifting of gears. My traditional theological friends had to go backwards because of their doctrine in order to function as credentialed chaplains. I felt advantaged in the formal chaplain training. Holmes Institute training for this work is close to none and with the Methodists and Presbyterians they have a whole training program. So one of the things I think we can do is to incorporate a formal chaplain training program.

REV. DR. DAVID BRUNNER
Senior minister, San Jose CSL, California

There are pivotal moments when I've had an "aha" moment, and one of them was with Dr. Margaret Stortz. I was ranting about something and I remember her saying, "Do you know that for a fact?"

"No."

"Then you best keep that to yourself."

Many things happened to me in that moment. It was a great turning point.

The thing I loved about working in GEMS is that I could work minister-to-minister, like, how can I assist you? What do I have that you need? When there was a need I would know how or find someone that knew the answers or how to do a specific job.

REV. DR. ARLEEN BUMP
Senior minister, past president (RSI), Ft. Lauderdale CSL, Florida

This conversation took place while I was president of RSI, in the mid-1990s, and talking with UCRS about a possible merger. Dr. Ruth Deaton and I got to like each other and we had a good time, but business-wise we were so far apart in terms of how we did things. Ruth and I were talking one day and we said, "You know what? This is a good idea, but it's not the right time."

REV. CYNTHIA CAVALCANTI
Ph.D., co-minister, Fremont CSL, California

Someone, someplace, is photocopying Science of Mind magazine for their friend, or Creative Thought for their friend. So what?! That's how we spread the word. The higher vision needs to be getting our teaching out into the world, print communication, whether that is paper-and-ink or electronic—it doesn't matter. It's a crucial vehicle; we can't do without it.

REV. DR. RUTH DEATON
Retired, served as president of UCRS, Director of GEMS, IBOT member, and leader of the Wisdom Council, Flagler Beach, Florida

Dr. Ruth Deaton and her husband Rev. Jack Deaton were instrumental in the training of very successful ministers, Revs. Jose and Alida Sosa of Monterrey, Mexico.

What I find so fascinating in Alida and Jose's classes is they will have doctors, lawyers, dentists, high professional men and women, and then when those men and women have patients or clients, they are in some way able to quietly refer Science of Mind principles to them. There have been a few incidents when a patient would wind up in the hospital and their family member would call Alida and Jose for treatment and a possible visit. Alida and Jose would see the patient, and do spiritual mind treatment, and the patient would get well. So, you know what happened? Alida and Jose were refused admittance to one or two of the hospitals because the doctors were so upset that the healing had happened. It was a loss of income.

REV. BARRY EBERT
Director of Youth, Mile Hi Church, Lakewood, Colorado

What I am really affirming for the movement is that we'll get more involved in youth education and getting kids connected through the truth of themselves early. I think we have done a fairly good job with teens along the way, but I'm really excited about our early childhood stuff and our elementary stuff and just getting families connected with our centers. That's something I've been working on a lot and feel really good about.

REV. DR. KENN GORDON
Community Spiritual Leader and co-minister at Kelowna CSL, B.C.

Dr. Kenn's first experience with Religious Science was the Palm Desert Church. That first Sunday, there was a guest speaker, Dr. Raymond Charles Barker. When he and his family returned the following week, the senior minister, Dr. Tom Costa, was back in his pulpit.

When I walked in he introduced himself. And when I walked out he remembered my name. So I was hooked. I loved what he had to say and he was so charismatic and so connected and so sweet. That was why he was called "Dr. Love."

[Editor's note: Dr. Costa was known to always remember a person's name even after not seeing him or her for several years. And, each week, he wrote notes by hand to new visitors.]

KATHY JULINE, RSCP
Former editor of Science of Mind magazine, San Clemente, California

While working for *Science of Mind* magazine, Kathy relates that her biggest challenge was switching from a typewriter to computer. She became the editor and has moved on to be one of our most prolific authors for the magazine (using a computer). In 2009, Kathy became a Practitioner.

Through practitioner training, I began to look carefully at areas of my life and to see where I was not experiencing or knowing the truth of oneness. Gradually, I let go of those barriers and began to see the Truth, that God is ever present, and that I am one with God. This has made a huge difference in my attitudes, in the things that I let myself think. In other words, if an old thought comes up that wants me, for example, to say, "Oh, that's too bad such and such happened," or "Oh gosh, that's going to be a problem," I can instantly stop myself and know that this is exactly God Presence in my life. And I can feel a sense of peace, a sense of deep trust, and I can simply flow harmoniously with whatever situation comes along, and remain at peace, and things just go beautifully. It's a humongous shift in attitude and consciousness. I no longer feel that sense of having to worry, or struggle or fret, because I feel guided; I feel safe.

REV. DR. ROGER JULINE
Semiretired, teaching and writing, San Clemente, California

On the subject of integration, Dr. Roger said,

I think the possibility of bringing all of this creative energy into one organization and getting a focus on what we want to do and how we want to develop and grow is going to enlarge the potential for all of us. I think too much energy in the past was spent saying "Well, we did this and RSI did that, and we do this and they do that." And now we're all going to be together. So I think it is right.

REV. DR. MAXINE KAYE
Author and never retired minister, California

Dr. Maxine graduated from ministerial classes in 1976. She has had a long and fruitful career, loving every moment.

I've been every kind of chaplain imaginable. I've been a hospice chaplain, a hospital chaplain. I did prison ministry. I put together a bereavement program in Palo Alto when I was there. I love all forms of chaplaincy. Dr. James Golden had also done all kinds of chaplaincy including police chaplaincy, and Dr. Carolyn McKeown was a policeman's and fireman's chaplain. So that, along with my favorite role for Board of Education as practitioner, and I am having a wonderful life full of love.

KEN LIND, RSCP
Former director of Science of Mind Foundation and interim editor for Science of Mind magazine, Minnesota

One of our largest donors was a woman named Camilla Devere, who lived in Pittsburg, Kansas. She had married an oil executive in California and was now widowed and comfortably well off. She had been a longtime student of Science of Mind and an avid reader of Science of Mind literature. I had such a delightful time visiting her. I was going to take her to dinner and I said, "You can pick the spot," and she picked a sort of crack in the wall, inside a mall, that served after hours. Nobody was there. She confirmed that this was where she wanted to eat. We had a sandwich. This was one of many wonderful experiences while raising money for the Science of Mind Foundation. Mrs. Devere gave nearly a half-million dollars in the form of charitable gift annuities. Another very generous woman was Marian Hefferlin, founder of the Dr. John Hefferlin and Marian Hefferlin Foundation.

The Cornerstone Campaign had been initiated to raise $5,000,000 for endowment and for furnishing for the new headquarters building. The campaign brought in $2,375,000 but never reached its goal. Bill Lynn was the executive director of the Cornerstone Foundation.

BILL LYNN
Business manager of the United Church for thirty-nine years, retired

The Cornerstone Foundation was really geared to raise money for education and one of the biggest concerns was around the School of Ministry. We didn't get off the ground. We did raise money and had a development program, but as far as the capital campaign, it just didn't work. Just about the time we were ready to ask the Board for approval for the start of the capital campaign, someone had the bright idea, I don't know who it was, to give the school of ministry away. Instead of solidifying and growing it, we were going to have several schools.

[Editor's note: Here we have two different stories about the Cornerstone Foundation and Campaign. They are probably both correct.]

REV. DR. HARRY MORGAN MOSES
Senior minister, SpiritWorks CSL, Burbank, California

We have an opportunity to build from a new place in consciousness, a new idea that will support the movement of the teaching into the world. That's what I'm dedicated to. Can we not make this available to more people in the world? If I didn't believe that as a result of being a practitioner of this Science of Mind for more than thirty years, my life was richer and more profound and more wonderful than anything I could imagine, I wouldn't teach this stuff.

REV. DR. JAY SCOTT NEALE
Co-minister, Fremont CSL, California

We are teaching people how to think critically about oneness—not about duality. Fortunately my teachers were insistent. Dr. Craig Carter was like a Zen master, he ran more people off. One of the main things I learned from Reginald Armor, was, "If you're moving into simplicity, you're going in the right direction; because the more we evolve into the understanding of Principle, the simpler it gets."

REV. DR. TOM SANNAR
Co-minister, One Spirit—One Mind, San Diego, California

The culture of the organization, the organic way that it was formed, it needed to have stability and order. It needed strong leadership. Then you get to this place from strong leadership to more democratic. Then when the power is supposedly in the field, that's where the power is, in the centers.

REV. DR. CHRISTIAN SORENSEN
Senior minister, Seaside CSL, Encinitas, California

I am very excited that in this era we have come together with integration. My concern is that the new organization has gone back to a decade ago—exactly what we spent a great deal of money, a great deal of time to eliminate—three heads of an organization. Granted that they have different roles, we have a president who is responsible for an organization, who may or may not be the chair of the board. Then you've got another leader and the community spiritual leader. But, with the people who are moving along with the integration I have zero concern. They absolutely understand. There is going to be no issue. My concern is in the next generation of leadership that the structure is set up so that we can once again return to a splitting of the power or the decision or where the buck stops.

[Editor's note: Historical note of interest—Dr. Sorensen entered ministerial school at the age of nineteen, becoming a minister in a pulpit at twenty-two.]

REV. DR. MARGARET STORTZ
Semiretired, author, guest speaker, El Cerrito, California

Of course this is highly subjective, and I have to acknowledge that there is some bias to it. Once upon a time I use to think I was a Religious Science moderate. Now I believe I have become a Religious Science conservative because I have felt that Religious Science, in order to be chic, in order to be timely, in order to be in the moment, and so forth, is, through some of the way it does things, shifting away from its roots. That's my major concern about the way they present themselves and the way they teach the coursework. I don't have any problem whatsoever with all the tangential courses to make it more interesting to look into more psychological work or other work. We've done that all along. I am concerned that they are moving away from the basic courses from their roots.

REV. DR. ROGER TEEL
Senior minister, Mile-Hi Church, Lakewood, Colorado

We went through phases where there was just a lot of ego-based conflict going on in the movement. I pray that we are ready to move on. I think we've been progressively growing. I still don't think we're clear on how we want to grow this thing. Hopefully, we shall be clear.

REV. DR. LLOYD TUPPER
Semiretired, guest speaker, San Francisco and Santa Barbara, California

In February 1968, Dr. Tupper heard Dr. Raymond Charles Barker speak in New York.

I was so blown over, so to speak, by this gentleman and his spiritual authority, the way he spoke, in the way he inspired, in the way he imparted a sense of unity and oneness in Spirit, of being, that we were all part of one infinite life, that life was God, that life was the infinite life that is Spirit, and that I was an individualization of that life which innately I had always known.

REV. DR. JOHN WATERHOUSE
Co-minister, Asheville CSL, North Carolina

An organization is a group of people, and they all have their ways. All of the idiosyncrasies and personality types make the organization. I have just fallen in love with this group; the people who are drawn to this teaching are extraordinary. They have a gift to insight, more so than any group of people I've ever known. As an organizational psychologist, I've studied from a clinical position how people work together. We're a group of people like any other in some sense, and in another sense we have extraordinary vision that we draw on. Though no one would say that Ernest Holmes was an organizational genius, he was, however, someone who could give a group of people his vision. And if they could see the vision, something extraordinary would happen.

About the Author

Marilyn Leo has been a part of Religious Science since childhood. Her father, Reginald Armor, was very close to Ernest Holmes, beginning in the year 1915, when he was a boy of twelve, and their families remained intimate throughout Holmes's life.

Marilyn has served on many committees and served United Church (now Centers for Spiritual Living) as Director of the World Ministry of Prayer, Ecclesiastical Officer/Vice President, Organizational Renewal Project, chair of the Global Core, as well as president, secretary, and treasurer (at different times) for the Wisdom Council (retired ministers' association). She has received several special recognitions including the "Living Treasure Award" given by her ministerial colleagues. In 2009, Marilyn received the "Golden Heart Award," also given by the United Clergy of Religious Science. United Church has honored her with honorary Doctor of Divinity and Doctor of Religious Science recognitions.

Though retired from the usual ministerial duties, she has served as president of the Science of Mind Archives and Library Foundation, and presently serves on the Board of Trustees for The Hefferlin Foundation, an independent non-profit foundation supporting the teaching of Science of Mind. In that capacity she is secretary of the board and co-chair of the Education/Scholarship Committee.

Besides her book *In His Company: Ernest Holmes Remembered,* she has written articles for the *Science of Mind* and *Creative Thought* magazines, contributed the manuscript for *That Was Ernest* written by her father, Dr. Reginald Armor, and published by DeVorss & Company. She compiled and edited *Love and Law* published by J. Tarcher/Putnam/Penguin, and she wrote the foreword for John Waterhouse's book *Five Steps to Freedom*, which, incidentally, has been translated to Spanish and Russian and has become required reading for some Science of Mind classes. It is also being created as an audiobook.

Marilyn has been working in the Religious Science Archives for fifteen years and created the Archives and Library Foundation, a nonprofit organization that houses all archival information for CSL. It is a "living archives" in that there are constantly additions being made. Visit the website at scienceofmindarchives.org.

Bibliography & References

Chapter 2

1. *Heaven Has No Favorites*. Unpublished manuscript by Reginald C. Armor.
2. "Minutes," page 1. December 10, 1926. Courtesy of Science of Mind Archives.
3. Ibid.
4. "Minutes," page 1. December 22, 1926. Courtesy of Science of Mind Archives.
5. Ibid.
6. Ibid.
7. "Minutes," page 1. January 5, 1927. Courtesy of Science of Mind Archives.
8. Ibid.
9. Ibid.
10. Ibid.
11. Ibid.
12. Ibid.
13. "Minutes," page 2. January 5, 1927. Courtesy of Science of Mind Archives.
14. "Meeting," page 1. January 12, 1927. Courtesy of Science of Mind Archives.
15. Ibid.
16. Ibid.
17. "Minutes of Organization Meeting of Board of Trustees of Institute of Religious Science and School of Philosophy," page 1. March 3, 1927. Courtesy of Science of Mind Archives.
18. "Minutes of Organization Meeting of Board of Trustees of Institute of Religious Science and School of Philosophy," page 2. March 3, 1927. Courtesy of Science of Mind Archives.
19. Ibid.
20. "Minutes of Organization Meeting of Board of Trustees of Institute of Religious Science and School of Philosophy," page 3. March 3, 1927. Courtesy of Science of Mind Archives.
21. "Minutes of the Regular Meeting of the Board of Trustees of the Institute of Religious Science, April 6, 1927," page 1. April 6, 1927. Courtesy of Science of Mind Archives.
22. Ibid.
23. "Minutes of the Regular Meeting of the Board of Trustees of the Institute of Religious Science, April 6, 1927," page 2. April 6, 1927. Courtesy of Science of Mind Archives.
24. "Minutes of May 4, 1927," page 1. May 4, 1927. Courtesy of Science of Mind Archives.
25. Ibid.
26. Ibid.
27. Ibid.
28. "Resolution Changing Principal Place of Business," page 1. June 1, 1927. Courtesy of Science of Mind Archives.
29. "Minutes for the Regular Monthly Meeting of the Institute of Religious Science and School of Philosophy," page 1. June 1, 1927. Courtesy of Science of Mind Archives.
30. "Minutes for the Regular Monthly Meeting of the Institute of Religious Science and School of Philosophy," page 1. July 6, 1927. Courtesy of Science of Mind Archives.
31. "Minutes for the Regular Monthly Meeting of the Institute of Religious Science and School of Philosophy," page 2. July 6, 1927. Courtesy of Science of Mind Archives.
32. Ibid.

33. Letter from Harrison Lewis to Mostyn Clinch, President of the Institute of Religious Science. July 11, 1927. Courtesy of Science of Mind Archives.

34. "Minutes for the Regular Monthly Meeting of the Institute of Religious Science and School of Philosophy," page 1. August 3, 1927. Courtesy of Science of Mind Archives.

35. Ibid.

36. "Minutes of the Regular Monthly Meeting of the Board of Trustees of the Institute of Religious Science and School of Philosophy," page 1. September 7, 1927. Courtesy of Science of Mind Archives.

37. "Minutes for the Regular Monthly Meeting of the Board of Trustees of the Institute of Religious Science and School of Philosophy," page 1. October 5, 1927. Courtesy of Science of Mind Archives.

38. "Minutes for the Regular Monthly Meeting of the Board of Trustees of the Institute of Religious Science and School of Philosophy," page 2. October 5, 1927. Courtesy of Science of Mind Archives.

39. "Minutes for the Regular Monthly Meeting of the Board of Trustees of the Institute of Religious Science and School of Philosophy," page 1. November 9, 1927. Courtesy of Science of Mind Archives.

40. "Minutes for the Regular Monthly Meeting of the Board of Trustees of the Institute of Religious Science and School of Philosophy," page 2. November 9, 1927. Courtesy of Science of Mind Archives.

41. "Minutes for the Regular Monthly Meeting of the Board of Trustees of the Institute of Religious Science and School of Philosophy," page 1. December 7, 1927. Courtesy of Science of Mind Archives.

42. "Minutes of the Regular Monthly Meeting of the Board of Trustees of the Institute of Religious Science and School of Philosophy," page 1. January 4, 1928. Courtesy of Science of Mind Archives.

43. Ibid.

44. "Minutes of the Regular Monthly Meeting of the Board of Trustees of the Institute of Religious Science and School of Philosophy," page 2. January 4, 1928. Courtesy of Science of Mind Archives.

45. Ibid.

46. Ibid.

47. Ibid.

48. "Minutes of the Regular Monthly Meeting of the Board of Trustees of the Institute of Religious Science and School of Philosophy," page 1. February 1, 1928. Courtesy of Science of Mind Archives.

49. "Minutes of the Regular Monthly Meeting of the Board of Trustees of the Institute of Religious Science and School of Philosophy," page 2. February 1, 1928. Courtesy of Science of Mind Archives.

50. Ibid.

51. "Minutes of the Regular Monthly Meeting of the Board of Trustees of the Institute of Religious Science and School of Philosophy," page 1. April 11, 1928. Courtesy of Science of Mind Archives.

52. "Minutes of the Regular Monthly Meeting of the Board of Trustees of the Institute of Religious Science and School of Philosophy," page 2. April 11, 1928. Courtesy of Science of Mind Archives.

53. Ibid.

54. Ibid.

55. Ibid.

56. "Minutes of the Regular Monthly Meeting of the Board of Trustees of the Institute of Religious Science and School of Philosophy," page 1. July 5, 1928. Courtesy of Science of Mind Archives.

57. "Minutes of the Regular Monthly Meeting of the Board of Trustees of the Institute of Religious Science," page 1. August 1, 1928. Courtesy of Science of Mind Archives.

58. "Minutes of the Regular Monthly Meeting of the Board of Trustees of the Institute of Religious Science," page 2. August 1, 1928. Courtesy of Science of Mind Archives.

59. "Minutes of the Regular Monthly Meeting of the Board of Trustees of the Institute of Religious Science," page 2. September 5, 1928. Courtesy of Science of Mind Archives.

60. Ibid.

61. "Minutes of the Regular Monthly Meeting of the Board of Trustees of the Institute of Religious Science," page 1. October 3, 1928. Courtesy of Science of Mind Archives.

62. "Minutes of the Special Meeting of the Board of Trustees of the Institute of Religious Science," page 1. September 28, 1928. Courtesy of Science of Mind Archives.

63. "Minutes of the Special Meeting of the Board of Trustees of the Institute of Religious Science," page 2. September 28, 1928. Courtesy of Science of Mind Archives.

64. "Minutes of the Regular Monthly Meeting of the Board of Trustees of the Institute of Religious Science," page 1. October 3, 1928. Courtesy of Science of Mind Archives.

65. "Minutes of the Regular Monthly Meeting of the Board of Trustees of the Institute of Religious Science," page 2. October 3, 1928. Courtesy of Science of Mind Archives.

66. "Minutes of the Regular Monthly Meeting of the Board of Trustees of the Institute of Religious Science," page 3. October 3, 1928. Courtesy of Science of Mind Archives.

67. Ibid.

68. Ibid.

69. "Minutes of the Regular Monthly Meeting of the Board of Trustees of the Institute of Religious Science," pages 1-2. November 7, 1928. Courtesy of Science of Mind Archives.

70. "Minutes of the Regular Monthly Meeting of the Board of Trustees of the Institute of Religious Science," page 1. December 5, 1928. Courtesy of Science of Mind Archives.

71. Ibid.

72. "Minutes of the Regular Monthly Meeting of the Board of Trustees of the Institute of Religious Science," page 1. January 9, 1929. Courtesy of Science of Mind Archives.

73. Ibid.

74. "Minutes of the Regular Monthly Meeting of the Board of Trustees of the Institute of Religious Science," page 1. February 6, 1929. Courtesy of Science of Mind Archives.

75. "Minutes of the Regular Monthly Meeting of the Board of Trustees of the Institute of Religious Science," page 2. February 6, 1929. Courtesy of Science of Mind Archives.

76. Ibid.

77. Ibid.

78. "Minutes of the Regular Monthly Meeting of the Board of Trustees of the Institute of Religious Science," page 3. February 6, 1929. Courtesy of Science of Mind Archives.

79. Ibid.

80. Ibid.

81. "Report of the Advisory Committee," page 3. February 25, 1929. Courtesy of Science of Mind Archives.

82. "Report of the Advisory Committee," pages 3-5. February 25, 1929. Courtesy of Science of Mind Archives.

83. "Minutes of the Regular Monthly Meeting of the Board of Trustees of the Institute of Religious Science," page 2. April 3, 1929. Courtesy of Science of Mind Archives.

84. Ibid.

85. Ibid.

86. "Minutes of the Regular Monthly Meeting of the Board of Trustees of the Institute of Religious Science," pages 1-2. May 8, 1929. Courtesy of Science of Mind Archives.

87. "Minutes of the Regular Monthly Meeting of the Board of Trustees of the Institute of Religious Science," pages 2-3. June 9, 1929. Courtesy of Science of Mind Archives.

88. "Minutes of the Meeting of the Board of Trustees of the Institute of Religious Science." June 30, 1929. Courtesy of Science of Mind Archives.

89. Ibid.

90. "Minutes of the Meeting of the Board of Trustees of the Institute of Religious Science." August 1929. Courtesy of Science of Mind Archives.

91. "Minutes of the Regular Monthly Meeting of the Board of Trustees of the Institute of Religious Science." October 1929. Courtesy of Science of Mind Archives.

92. "Minutes of the Regular Monthly Meeting of the Board of Trustees of the Institute of Religious Science," page 1. September 11, 1929. Courtesy of Science of Mind Archives.

93. Ibid.

94. *Religious Science: A Magazine of Christian Philosophy.* October 1927. Institute of Religious Science and School of Philosophy. Courtesy of Science of Mind Archives. Cover page and inside front cover.

95. *Religious Science: A Magazine of Christian Philosophy.* October 1927. Institute of Religious Science and School of Philosophy. Courtesy of Science of Mind Archives. Page 2.

96. Ibid.

97. Ibid.

98. *Religious Science: A Magazine of Christian Philosophy.* October 1927. Institute of Religious Science and School of Philosophy. Courtesy of Science of Mind Archives. Page 21.

99. *Religious Science: A Magazine of Christian Philosophy.* October 1927. Institute of Religious Science and School of Philosophy. Courtesy of Science of Mind Archives. Page 31.

100. Ibid.

101. *Religious Science: A Magazine of Christian Philosophy.* October 1927. Institute of Religious Science and School of Philosophy. Courtesy of Science of Mind Archives. Page 32.

102. *Religious Science: A Magazine of Christian Philosophy.* October 1927. Institute of Religious Science and School of Philosophy. Courtesy of Science of Mind Archives. Page 33.

CHAPTER 3

1. Barker, Raymond Charles. (1968). *The Power of Decision: A Step-by-Step Program to Overcome Indecision and Live Without Failure Forever.* New York: Jeremy P. Tarcher/Penguin. Page 197.

2. Holmes, Ernest S. (1926, rev. ed. 2010). *The Science of Mind.* New York: Tarcher/Penguin. Page 145.

3. *The Science of Mind Magazine.* January 1930. Institute of Religious Science and School of Philosophy. Front cover. Courtesy of Science of Mind Archives.

4. *The Science of Mind Magazine.* January 1930. Institute of Religious Science and School of Philosophy. Inside front cover. Courtesy of Science of Mind Archives.

5. Ibid.

6. *The Science of Mind Magazine.* January 1930. Institute of Religious Science and School of Philosophy. Page 1. Courtesy of Science of Mind Archives.

7. *The Science of Mind Magazine.* January 1930. Institute of Religious Science and School of Philosophy. Page 49. Courtesy of Science of Mind Archives.

8. *The Science of Mind Magazine.* January 1930. Institute of Religious Science and School of Philosophy. Back cover. Courtesy of Science of Mind Archives.

9. "Minutes of the Regular Meeting of the Board of Trustees of the Institute of Religious Science and Philosophy, Inc.," page 1. June 11, 1930. Courtesy of Science of Mind Archives.

10. Ibid.

11. "Minutes of the Regular Meeting of the Board of Trustees of the Institute of Religious Science and Philosophy, Inc.," page 2. June 11, 1930. Courtesy of Science of Mind Archives.

12. "Minutes of the Regular Meeting of the Board of Trustees of the Institute of Religious Science and Philosophy, Inc.," page 3. July 9, 1930. Courtesy of Science of Mind Archives.

13. "Minutes of the Regular Meeting of the Board of Trustees of the Institute of Religious Science and School of Philosophy, Inc.," page 2. October 8, 1930. Courtesy of Science of Mind Archives.

14. "Minutes of the Regular Meeting of the Board of Trustees of the Institute of Religious Science and School of Philosophy, Inc.," page 2. November 12, 1930. Courtesy of Science of Mind Archives.

15. "Minutes of the Special Meeting of the Board of Trustees of the Institute of Religious Science and School of Philosophy, Inc.," pages 1–2. December 18, 1930. Courtesy of Science of Mind Archives.

16. *Quarterly Journal of Science, Religion, and Philosophy.* 1930. Vol. 1, No. 1. Table of contents. Courtesy of Science of Mind Archives.

17. *Quarterly Journal of Science, Religion, and Philosophy.* 1931. Vol. 2, No. 3. Courtesy of Science of Mind Archives.

18. Ibid.

19. Ibid.

20. "Minutes of the Regular Meeting of the Board of Trustees of the Institute of Religious Science and School of Philosophy, Inc.," page 2. March 11, 1931. Courtesy of Science of Mind Archives.

21. "Minutes of the Regular Meeting of the Board of Trustees of the Institute of Religious Science and School of Philosophy, Inc.," page 4. October 14, 1931. Courtesy of Science of Mind Archives.

22. "Minutes of the Regular Meeting of the Board of Trustees of The Institute of Religious Science and School of Philosophy, Inc.," page 4. November 13, 1931. Courtesy of Science of Mind Archives.

23. "Minutes of the Regular Meeting of the Board of Trustees of The Institute of Religious Science and School of Philosophy, Inc.," page 2. November 13, 1931. Courtesy of Science of Mind Archives.

24. "1932 Budget for the Institute," pages 1–2. December 1931. Courtesy of Science of Mind Archives.

25. "Minutes of the Regular Meeting of the Board of Trustees of the Institute of Religious Science and School of Philosophy, Inc.," page 5. May 12, 1932. Courtesy of Science of Mind Archives.

26. "Minutes of the Regular Meeting of the Board of Trustees of the Institute of Religious Science and School of Philosophy, Inc.," page 2. February 11, 1936. Courtesy of Science of Mind Archives.

27. "Minutes of the Regular Meeting of the Board of Trustees of the Institute of Religious Science and School of Philosophy, Inc.," page 1. September 1936. Courtesy of Science of Mind Archives.

28. "Minutes of the Regular Meeting of the Board of Trustees of the Institute of Religious Science and Philosophy," page 1. October 13, 1936. Courtesy of Science of Mind Archives.

29. Ibid.

30. Ibid.

31. "Minutes of the Regular Meeting of the Board of Trustees of the Institute of Religious Science & Philosophy," page 1. April 18, 1939. Courtesy of Science of Mind Archives.

32. "Minutes of the Meeting of the Board of Trustees of the Institute of Religious Science & Philosophy." May 16, 1939. Courtesy of Science of Mind Archives.

CHAPTER 4

1. Holmes, Ernest. (1934, rev. ed. 1941). *The Ebell Lectures on Spiritual Science.* Los Angeles: De Vorss & Co. Page 50.

2. "Minutes of the Meeting of the Board of Trustees of the Institute of Religious Science & Philosophy," page 2. September 16, 1941. Courtesy of Science of Mind Archives.

3. Ibid.

4. "Minutes of the Meeting of the Board of Trustees of the Institute of Religious Science & Philosophy," page 1. October 2, 1941. Courtesy of Science of Mind Archives.

5. "Minutes of the Special Meeting of the Board of Trustees of the Institute of Religious Science & Philosophy," page 1. October 14, 1941. Courtesy of Science of Mind Archives.

6. "Minutes of the Meeting of the Board of Trustees of the Institute of Religious Science & Philosophy," page 1. October 17, 1941. Courtesy of Science of Mind Archives.

7. Ibid.

8. "Minutes of the Meeting of the Board of Trustees of the Institute of Religious Science & Philosophy," page 1. November 18, 1941. Courtesy of Science of Mind Archives.

9. "Minutes of the Meeting of the Board of Trustees of the Institute of Religious Science & Philosophy," page 1. April 5, 1945. Courtesy of Science of Mind Archives.

10. "Minutes of the Meeting of the Board of Trustees of the Institute of Religious Science & Philosophy," page 2. May 16, 1945. Courtesy of Science of Mind Archives.

11. "Minutes of the Meeting of the Board of Trustees of the Institute of Religious Science & Philosophy," page 1. May 22, 1945. Courtesy of Science of Mind Archives.

12. "Minutes of the Meeting of the Board of Trustees of the Institute of Religious Science & Philosophy," page 1. June 20, 1945. Courtesy of Science of Mind Archives.

13. "Minutes of the Meeting of the Board of Trustees of the Institute of Religious Science & Philosophy," page 1. September 19, 1945. Courtesy of Science of Mind Archives.

14. "Minutes of the Meeting of the Board of Trustees of the Institute of Religious Science & Philosophy," page 2. October 17, 1945. Courtesy of Science of Mind Archives.

15. "Minutes of the Meeting of the Board of Trustees of the Institute of Religious Science & Philosophy," page 3. October 17, 1945. Courtesy of Science of Mind Archives.

16. "Minutes of the Meeting of the Board of Trustees of the Institute of Religious Science & Philosophy," pages 1-2. November 21, 1945. Courtesy of Science of Mind Archives.

17. "Minutes of the Meeting of the Board of Trustees of the Institute of Religious Science & Philosophy," pages 2-3. December 19, 1945. Courtesy of Science of Mind Archives.

18. "Minutes of the Meeting of the Board of Trustees of the Institute of Religious Science & Philosophy," page 1. February 20, 1946. Courtesy of Science of Mind Archives.

19. "Minutes of the Meeting of the Board of Trustees of the Institute of Religious Science & Philosophy," page 2. February 20, 1946. Courtesy of Science of Mind Archives.

20. "Regular Meeting of the Southern California Association of Chapters of the Institute of Religious Science," pages 1-3. May 13, 1946. Courtesy of Science of Mind Archives.

21. Ibid.

22. Ibid.

23. "Minutes of the Meeting of the Board of Trustees of the Institute of Religious Science & Philosophy," page 2. May 15, 1946. Courtesy of Science of Mind Archives.

24. "Minutes of the Meeting of the Board of Trustees of the Institute of Religious Science & Philosophy," page 3. May 15, 1946. Courtesy of Science of Mind Archives.

25. "Minutes of the Meeting of the Board of Trustees of the Institute of Religious Science & Philosophy," page 4. May 15, 1946. Courtesy of Science of Mind Archives.

26. "Minutes of the Meeting of the Board of Trustees of the Institute of Religious Science & Philosophy," page 1. June 11, 1946. Courtesy of Science of Mind Archives.

27. "Minutes of the Meeting of the Board of Trustees of the Institute of Religious Science & Philosophy," page 2. June 11, 1946. Courtesy of Science of Mind Archives.

28. "Minutes of the Meeting of the Board of Trustees of the Institute of Religious Science & Philosophy," page 1. June 11, 1946. Courtesy of Science of Mind Archives.

29. "Minutes of the Meeting of the Board of Trustees of the Institute of Religious Science & Philosophy," pages 2-3. September 18, 1946. Courtesy of Science of Mind Archives.

30. "Minutes of the Meeting of the Board of Trustees of the Institute of Religious Science & Philosophy," page 3. September 18, 1946. Courtesy of Science of Mind Archives.

31. "Minutes of the Meeting of the Board of Trustees of the Institute of Religious Science & Philosophy," page 1. August 13, 1947. Courtesy of Science of Mind Archives.

32. "Minutes of the Meeting of the Board of Trustees of the Institute of Religious Science & Philosophy," page 2. September 17, 1947. Courtesy of Science of Mind Archives.

33. "Minutes of the Meeting of the Board of Trustees of the Institute of Religious Science & Philosophy," page 3. September 17, 1947. Courtesy of Science of Mind Archives.

34. "Minutes of the Meeting of the Board of Trustees of the Institute of Religious Science & Philosophy," page 1. November 19, 1947. Courtesy of Science of Mind Archives.

35. Ibid.

36. "Sixth Annual Meeting of the Religious Chapter Association, Program." January 26-27, 1948. Courtesy of Science of Mind Archives.

37. Ibid.

38. Ibid.

39. "Minutes of the Meeting of the Board of Trustees of the Institute of Religious Science & Philosophy," page 1. March 24, 1949. Courtesy of Science of Mind Archives.

40. Ibid.

41. Letter from Reginald C. Armor to Dr. Bitzer. Page 1. September 6, 1949. Courtesy of Science of Mind Archives.

42. Letter from Charles Kinnear to Chapter Leaders. Page 1. January 26, 1949. Courtesy of Science of Mind Archives.

CHAPTER 5

1. Troward, Thomas. (1909). *The Doré Lectures on Mental Science.* New York: Dodd, Mead, & Company. Page 25.

2. "International Association of Religious Science Churches Meeting of Representative Council," page 1. February 13, 1950. Courtesy of Science of Mind Archives.

3. "International Association of Religious Science Churches Meeting of Representative Council," page 2. March 13, 1950. Courtesy of Science of Mind Archives.

4. "Minutes of the Meeting of the Board of Trustees of the Institute of Religious Science & Philosophy," page 1. February 23, 1950. Courtesy of Science of Mind Archives.

5. "Minutes of the Meeting of the Board of Trustees of the Institute of Religious Science & Philosophy," pages 1-2. March 23, 1950. Courtesy of Science of Mind Archives.

6. "Minutes of the Meeting of the Board of Trustees of the Institute of Religious Science & Philosophy," page 1. April 27, 1950. Courtesy of Science of Mind Archives.

7. Ibid.

8. "International Association of Religious Science Churches Meeting of Representative Council," page 2. May 5, 1950. Courtesy of Science of Mind Archives.

9. "Letter from Fletcher A. Harding, D.R.S. to All Chartered Religious Science Churches," page 1. October 5, 1950. Courtesy of Science of Mind Archives.

10. "Minutes of the Meeting of the Board of Trustees of the Institute of Religious Science & Philosophy," page 1. June 22, 1950. Courtesy of Science of Mind Archives.

11. "Minutes of the Meeting of the Board of Trustees of the Institute of Religious Science & Philosophy," page 1. July 20, 1950. Courtesy of Science of Mind Archives.

12. "Minutes of the Meeting of the Board of Trustees of the Institute of Religious Science & Philosophy," page 1. September 21, 1950. Courtesy of Science of Mind Archives.

13. "Minutes of the Meeting of the Board of Trustees of the Institute of Religious Science & Philosophy," page 1. October 19, 1950. Courtesy of Science of Mind Archives.

14. Ibid.

15. "Minutes of the Meeting of the Board of Trustees of the Institute of Religious Science & Philosophy," page 1. December 21, 1950. Courtesy of Science of Mind Archives.

16. Ibid.

17. Ibid.

18. "Minutes of the Meeting of the Board of Trustees of the Institute of Religious Science & Philosophy," page 1. February 15, 1951. Courtesy of Science of Mind Archives.

19. Ibid.

20. "Minutes of the Meeting of the Board of Trustees of the Institute of Religious Science & Philosophy," page 2. March 15, 1951. Courtesy of Science of Mind Archives.

21. "Minutes of the Meeting of the Board of Trustees of the Institute of Religious Science & Philosophy," page 1. April 19, 1951. Courtesy of Science of Mind Archives.

22. "Minutes of the Meeting of the Board of Trustees of the Institute of Religious Science & Philosophy," page 1. May 3, 1951. Courtesy of Science of Mind Archives.

23. "International Association of Religious Science Churches Meeting of Representative Council," page 1. October 14, 1951. Courtesy of Science of Mind Archives.

24. Ibid.

25. "Minutes of the Meeting of the Board of Trustees of the Institute of Religious Science & Philosophy," page 1. July 26, 1951. Courtesy of Science of Mind Archives.

26. "International Association of Religious Science Churches Meeting of Representative Council," page 1. August 5, 1951. Courtesy of Science of Mind Archives.

27. Ibid.

28. "Minutes of the Meeting of the Board of Trustees of the Institute of Religious Science & Philosophy," page 1. November 29, 1951. Courtesy of Science of Mind Archives.

29. Ibid.

30. Ibid.

31. "International Association of Religious Science Churches Meeting of Representative Council," page 1. December 10, 1951. Courtesy of Science of Mind Archives.

32. Interview with Dr. Frank Richelieu by Dr. Marilyn Leo.

33. "Minutes of the Meeting of the Board of Trustees of the Institute of Religious Science & Philosophy," pages 1-2. February 28, 1952. Courtesy of Science of Mind Archives.

34. "Minutes of the Meeting of the Board of Trustees of the Institute of Religious Science & Philosophy," page 3. February 28, 1952. Courtesy of Science of Mind Archives.

35. Ibid.

36. "Minutes of the Meeting of the Board of Trustees of the Institute of Religious Science & Philosophy," page 1. March 27, 1952. Courtesy of Science of Mind Archives.

37. "Minutes of the Meeting of the Board of Trustees of the Institute of Religious Science & Philosophy," page 2. May 22, 1952. Courtesy of Science of Mind Archives.

38. "Minutes of the Meeting of the Board of Trustees of the Institute of Religious Science & Philosophy," page 2. September 25, 1952. Courtesy of Science of Mind Archives.

39. "Minutes of the Meeting of the Board of Trustees of the Institute of Religious Science & Philosophy," page 1. October 23, 1952. Courtesy of Science of Mind Archives.

40. "Minutes of the Meeting of the Board of Trustees of the Institute of Religious Science & Philosophy," page 1. November 20, 1952. Courtesy of Science of Mind Archives.

41. Ibid.

42. "International Association of Religious Science Churches Meeting of Representative Council," page 1. January 4, 1953. Courtesy of Science of Mind Archives.

43. "International Association of Religious Science Churches Meeting of Representative Council," pages 2-3. January 16, 1953. Courtesy of Science of Mind Archives.

44. Ibid.

45. Interview with William Lynn by Dr. Marilyn Leo, 2011.

46. "Special Meeting of the Board of Trustees of the Institute of Religious Science & Philosophy," page 1. December 4, 1953. Courtesy of Science of Mind Archives.

47. "Minutes of the Meeting of the Board of Trustees of the Institute of Religious Science & Philosophy," page 1. December 29, 1953. Courtesy of Science of Mind Archives.

48. Ibid.

49. "Minutes of the Meeting of the Board of Trustees of the Institute of Religious Science & Philosophy," pages 2-3. December 29, 1953. Courtesy of Science of Mind Archives.

50. Holmes, Ernest. (1934, rev. ed. 1941). *The Ebell Lectures on Spiritual Science*. Los Angeles: De Vorss & Co. Page 28.

51. "Meeting of the Representative Council," page 1. January 6, 1954. Courtesy of Science of Mind Archives.

52. "Meeting of the Representative Council," pages 1-2. January 6, 1954. Courtesy of Science of Mind Archives.

53. "Meeting of the Representative Council," page 2. January 6, 1954. Courtesy of Science of Mind Archives.

54. Ibid.

55. "Meeting of the Representative Council," page 1. January 7, 1954. Courtesy of Science of Mind Archives.

56. Ibid.

57. "Meeting of the Representative Council," page 1. January 8, 1954. Courtesy of Science of Mind Archives.

58. Minutes of the 1954 Convention. Pages 14-15. Courtesy of Science of Mind Archives.

59. Minutes of the 1954 Convention. Pages 15-16. Courtesy of Science of Mind Archives.

60. Minutes of the 1954 Convention. Page 16. Courtesy of Science of Mind Archives.

61. Minutes of the 1954 Convention. Pages 17-18. Courtesy of Science of Mind Archives.

62. Minutes of the 1954 Convention. Page 18. Courtesy of Science of Mind Archives.

63. Ibid.

64. Minutes of the 1954 Convention. Pages 18-20. Courtesy of Science of Mind Archives.

65. Minutes of the 1954 Convention. Pages 20-21. Courtesy of Science of Mind Archives.

66. Minutes of the 1954 Convention. Page 21. Courtesy of Science of Mind Archives.

67. Minutes of the 1954 Convention. Pages 21-22. Courtesy of Science of Mind Archives.

68. Minutes of the 1954 Convention. Page 23. Courtesy of Science of Mind Archives.

69. Minutes of the 1954 Convention. Pages 23-24. Courtesy of Science of Mind Archives.

70. Interview with Dr. Frank Richelieu by Dr. Marilyn Leo.

71. "Minutes of the Meeting of the Board of Trustees of the Church of Religious Science," page 1. January 28, 1954. Courtesy of Science of Mind Archives.

72. Ibid.

73. Ibid.

74. Ibid.

75. "Minutes of the I.A.R.S.C. Special Congress," page 1. May 20-21, 1954. Courtesy of Science of Mind Archives.

76. "Minutes of the I.A.R.S.C. Special Congress," pages 1-2. May 20-21, 1954. Courtesy of Science of Mind Archives.

77. Ibid.

78. "Minutes of the 1955 Annual Convention of the Church of Religious Science," page 1. January 3-6, 1955. Courtesy of Science of Mind Archives.

79. Ibid.

80. "Minutes of the 1955 Annual Convention of the Church of Religious Science," pages 1-2. January 3-6, 1955. Courtesy of Science of Mind Archives.

81. "Minutes of the 1955 Annual Convention of the Church of Religious Science," page 2. January 3-6, 1955. Courtesy of Science of Mind Archives.

82. Ibid.

83. Ibid.

84. "Minutes of the 1955 Annual Convention of the Church of Religious Science," page 3. January 3-6, 1955. Courtesy of Science of Mind Archives.

85. Ibid.

86. Ibid.

87. Ibid.

88. "Minutes of the 1955 Annual Convention of the Church of Religious Science," page 4. January 3-6, 1955. Courtesy of Science of Mind Archives.

89. Ibid.

90. "Minutes of the 1955 Annual Convention of the Church of Religious Science," page 5. January 3-6, 1955. Courtesy of Science of Mind Archives.
91. Ibid.
92. Ibid.
93. Ibid.
94. "Minutes of the 1955 Annual Convention of the Church of Religious Science," page 6. January 3-6, 1955. Courtesy of Science of Mind Archives.
95. Ibid.
96. Ibid.
97. Holmes, Ernest. (1948). *This Thing Called Life*. New York: Dodd, Mead, & Company. Page 30.
98. Interview with William Lynn by Dr. Marilyn Leo, 2011.
99. "Board of Directors of the I.A.R.S.C.," page 1. January 16, 1956. Courtesy of Science of Mind Archives.
100. "Board of Directors of the I.A.R.S.C.," page 1. March 12, 1956. Courtesy of Science of Mind Archives.
101. "Executive Committee Meeting," page 1. September 6, 1956. Courtesy of Science of Mind Archives.
102. Ibid.
103. "Board of Directors Meeting of the I.A.R.S.C.," page 1. November 12, 1956. Courtesy of Science of Mind Archives.
104. "Board of Directors Meeting of the I.A.R.S.C.," page 2. November 12, 1956. Courtesy of Science of Mind Archives.
105. "Board of Directors Meeting of the I.A.R.S.C.," page 3. November 12, 1956. Courtesy of Science of Mind Archives.
106. "I.A.R.S.C. Board of Directors Meeting," page 2. January 7, 1957. Courtesy of Science of Mind Archives.
107. Interview with Rev. Cay Thompson by Dr. Marilyn Leo, July 2011.
108. Interview with Dorothy Procopenko by Dr. Marilyn Leo, May 2011.
109. "Meeting of the Board of Directors of the I.A.R.S.C.," page 1. September 23, 1957. Courtesy of Science of Mind Archives.
110. "Executive Committee Meeting of the I.A.R.S.C.," page 1. December 2, 1957. Courtesy of Science of Mind Archives.
111. Ibid.
112. Letter from Ernest Holmes to Raymond Barker, May 27, 1958. Courtesy of Science of Mind Archives.
113. Letter from Ernest Holmes to Raymond Barker, August 18, 1959. Courtesy of Science of Mind Archives.
114. Leo, Richard. (1984). *A History of United Clergy of Religious Science*. Unpublished manuscript.

Index

R

Radio broadcast [Twelve Lessons on the Fundamentals of Religious Science] 26–27
Radio Corporation of America (RCA) 87
Radio Fund 68
Raven, Marjorie 124
Reed, Walter 136
Robinson, Frank 57–59, 85
Rubin, Sue 4
Ruckman, Estelle 71
Rundel, Augusta "Gussie" 26, 30, 52
Ruskin Art Club 38

S

San Francisco Church of Religious Science 88–89
Sannar, Tom 13, 147
Scanlan, E. J. 90, 95
Schofield, Anita 60, 77
Schubert, Denise 5
Scientology 80
Seymour, Ada 41
Shedd, John 48
Shelhamer, Ivy 60, 73
Shipman, Ann 20
Sills, Milton 54–56
Sindon, Geoffrey 3, 13, 16
Skok, Paul 13
Slonaker, C. E. 35
Smith, Alberta 39, 41, 56
Smith, Frank 35
Sorensen, Christian 147
Sosa, Jose and Alida 142
Spear, Harold 28–29
Stauffacher, A. D. 48
Stewart, Carroll 35
Stortz, Margaret 141, 147
Sutton, Marcia 7
Sykes, Fred 95

T

Taylor, Layne 3
Taylor, Maye 41
Teel, Roger 148
Temple, C. Warren 39
Temple Emanu-El 50–51
Thompson, Cay 130
Time Theater 65
Timmers, Frankie 5
Toole, Gregory 6–8, 10, 15
Torkelson, Andy 12
Trattner, Ernest 46, 48, 73
Trine, Ralph Waldo 77
Troward, Thomas 41, 46, 75
Trowbridge, Carmelita 60, 95, 104, 113
Tubbs, William 60
Tucker, Tammi 5
Tuckman, Ralph 136
Tupper, Lloyd 148
Turk, Iris 95–96
Turrell, Jim 4, 11
Twyne, J. Arthur 60

U

United Nations 79
Uptown Theater 79, 83
Usher, Geraldine 61

V

Van Slyke, Helen 26, 39, 44, 46
Van Valkenburgh, Norman 80, 88, 117
Vinek, Jeanette 3
Violet, Leslie 73
Vogt, June Kelly 137

W

Waddel, Leigh 10, 16
Wade, Madalyn 4
Wade, Martin 48
Walker, David 4

Made in the USA
Lexington, KY
16 October 2013